Kathleen
You're wonderful!
Proud if you.

Cin Stm

UTMOST LIVING

ALSO BY TIM STOREY

It's Time for Your Comeback

UTMOST
Living

Creating and Savoring
Your Best Life Now

TIM STOREY

Harmony Books

NEW YORK

All rights reserved.

Published in the United States by Harmony Books, an imprint of the
Crown Publishing Group, a division of Random House, Inc., New York.
www.crownpublishing.com

Harmony Books is a registered trademark and the Harmony Books colophon
is a trademark of Random House, Inc.

Library of Congress Cataloging-in-Publication Data
Storey, Tim.
Utmost living : creating and savoring your best life now / Tim Storey.
p.   cm.
1. Self-actualization (Psychology)   2. Success.   I. Title.
BF637.S8S6995   2008
158.1—dc22   2007043359

ISBN 978-0-307-34177-8

Printed in the United States of America

Design by Lynne Amft

10   9   8   7   6   5   4   3

First Edition

To my older brother, Randy

1957–2000

From bunk-bed roommate to sharing hand-me-down clothes . . . even though your journey was sometimes difficult, you instilled in me a drive to succeed. Thank you for protecting me and believing in me while I was just a little kid with a big Afro and a pocketful of dreams.

Contents

UTMOST LIVING

Introduction

It is time to design the life that feeds the real you, the person with a dream craving to be fulfilled. By opening this book, you have started on the path to your utmost life. Some people ask me what I mean by that, and it's really very simple. An utmost life is the opposite of an "almost" life—you know, the life of people who *almost* take advantage of the abilities and skills they were given. An utmost life reaches beyond a "mostly" life: the world of those people who *mostly* have what they want and achieve what they can, but don't really jump up to being as outstanding as they could be.

You are one of the people who want to live an utmost life—a life in which you achieve everything you've hoped for, realize all the dreams you can dream, give back to the world as much as you've been given, and remain richer than ever. I know you can do it. I want to help.

My life and my work are based on the principle that we should always be looking for ways to nourish our spirit as well as we nourish our bodies. The search for the ingredients, the tools, and the techniques that can harvest life's abundant riches has always been an important part of my life. In this book, I have tried to combine and distill my studies of the spirit, the world, and the lives of profound thinkers, great benefactors, and strong leaders, as well as my experiences in helping people overcome challenges and fears both large and small. In this book, I will share some of the principles I have learned that will unlock the doors to a better tomorrow for you.

This book offers clear and specific recipes to help you make decisions that will empower you to live a rewarding, productive, "no regrets" life. As a life coach to many well-known athletes and entertainment celebrities, I have seen a similar longing in everyone I counsel, and I would guess that you have it too. You have a dream in you that longs to be fulfilled. Stop, look, and listen to your inner voice—it's telling you what you would rather be doing.

You may have come to this book because of a specific objective you want to accomplish, such as quitting smoking or getting a better job. I can help there. You may have a troubling problem in your life that you want to solve—something that is ruining your health or damaging your relationships. I can help there too. You may have come to this book because of a general feeling that your life is lacking something, a belief that there must be something better to do with your time. I can help you there.

Even if you've accomplished those goals and overcome those problems, there is still something more that this book can do for you. For this is a book about utmost living—creating a life that does honor not only to yourself but also to the people and the world around you. It's a book about a life that is constantly growing and giving back. It's about an utmost life. It's a book that you may never finish, no more than your life is ever finished. It's about a marvelous journey through a rich and rewarding country that is called your life. Let's take a look at it.

It's Not What You've Got, It's How You Use It

Without ever having met you, I can tell you that you have all the abilities you need to become a world shaker and a history maker. It's all in how you marshal them to the task and learn to take advantage of the gifts in yourself. That is what makes you special, and in order for you to become great, you will have to use your unique style and talents. That's what makes you different from everyone else in the world.

I've had the privilege of traveling to fifty-five of the world's countries, and forty-eight of the U.S. states. As soon as I arrive at my latest destination, I search for the local diner. Of course, that's not what it's called everywhere—in France it's a café and in England a pub—but every country has them, the places where people come for a satisfying, casual meal, a little conversation, and a comfortable atmosphere. The diners of the world have become a haven to me, but what's more, I believe the way we act in a diner can tell us a lot about the rest of our lives.

For instance, the first thing we have to do in a diner is to make a decision—where to sit. That may sound trivial, but it's not: everyday choices matter. Have you ever really thought about the choices you make every day? Life is full of tantalizing options and sometimes difficult decisions. The way you make decisions in a diner may reflect the way you live the rest of your life. Do you carefully choose what to eat, looking for the foods that will keep you healthy and energetic, always prepared for new challenges? Do you just take the first thing that looks appetizing? Do you let other people decide what you should eat?

If a waiter seems rushed to take your order, do you readily comply, ordering what you always have when you eat there? Do you ever say, "I need more time to look at the menu"? If you aren't thinking carefully about what goes into your body, you may be rushing through other decisions about what goes into your life too.

But they will always lead to consequences, whether it's the occasional bout of indigestion or a chronic heartburn that robs you of the simple pleasure of eating. For example, that burger and supersized fries that we continue to order for lunch each day can add unwanted pounds that stay on our bellies for years. But I'm not really talking about the burger and fries. It's the fact that we don't think about what the end result will be twenty years later—a heart attack. A decision you make once and never think about again can result in a lifetime of regret. You may have decided years ago to give up on a long-term dream for a short-term advantage—and now, after all that time, you wonder why your life seems so purposeless. Your dream had a coronary.

This book is about choosing *on purpose* the life we want to lead, and learning how to find it. Just as we have to decide what to eat every day, we should be deciding how to live every day. *Every* choice we make influences the quality of our lives—and decisions made quickly have lingering results.

But I don't mean that you should be agonizing over every bite or trying to decide if it's the right moment to get out of bed. Just as there are some basic principles about what foods are good for us, there are basic principles about how to live life to the utmost. With these principles, you will develop habits of acting and thinking and living that will transform your life. I want to give you the guidelines that will make your life fully satisfying and richly rewarding—not just for you but for everyone around you.

Now Is the Time to Be Great

Choices matter every day. Don't choose the same menu item each time if you want your life to be different from what it was yesterday. You will regret quick decisions that do not prepare you for utmost living. You may have been ordering the same sausage and mushroom thin-crust pizza week after week, even year after year, but have never stopped to think why life seems dull, dreary, and boring. Or even worse, perhaps you don't decide at all—perhaps you are letting someone else plan your menu each day.

After only a few pages of this book, you will see how the neighborhood diner offers rich lessons in how to make good choices in life's diner. You will be able to see how the choices you make in life will leave you satisfied or wanting more. You can live a healthy life or a wasted, overindulged life; you can even starve yourself. All the options are yours for the choosing.

I'm an ordained minister as well as a life coach, so God is essential to everything I do. You may think of God in a different way, or you may not think of God very much at all. I believe that God is real and can make your life infinitely easier with His strength. But if your faith is expressed in a different way, we can still talk. You may not believe that His purpose was to create our life and our lives, but you can still want to fulfill your purpose for your life. As long as you believe in yourself, we can do great things together.

But I am telling you that life offers wonderful options, and those options add seasoning to your life. Just because your life has taken on a certain shape and rhythm doesn't mean that is the way it always has to be. Your life can taste good again. Once you start reading this book, keep it with you until you finish it.

Each chapter will challenge you to pause and digest this food for thought before rushing back to your daily activities. Every chapter provides a "take-home bag," a place to write down your dreams and carry them with you for your next meal.

I'm going to make you work in this book, but you'll be working on yourself. Have you ever really taken the time to get to know yourself— know yourself beyond all the things you feel guilty about, the things you can't help doing, the duties you feel bound to carry out? Well, you are not just a haphazard collection of failures, weaknesses, duties, responsibilities, and rules. You are a person of real worth, you have value in this world, and you can add value to this world.

Our work will involve both clarifying who you are and creating guides for your actions. You could call it making a recipe for the life you want to live. You will need to make a record of what you're doing both to keep you focused and to show you how you've improved. Writing is probably the best way to do that, but you may be more comfortable and more productive keeping your record another way. Maybe you record notes on your cell phone. However you do it, be sure to do it. At the end of each chapter, I've offered some pages to help you envision your utmost life and find ways to achieve it. Your utmost life will be different from anyone else's, and the way you achieve it will be different from anyone else's. What's important is that you keep a record of the journey.

I'm offering you different ways to start—questions and other aids to help you think, if you need them. Take advantage of the ones that are useful to you, but don't feel you have to answer every question or fill in every blank. What's here is not a test. Think of it more as a collection of coaching tips that will help you not just make the most of what you have but achieve the unlimited potential that exists within you.

As I say in the book, you will always be accomplishing goals and dreaming new dreams. I hope you will find the pages at the end of each chapter useful over and over again, so you might want to photocopy them. The only thing you can't do is not do. I'll say here for the first time, but not the last, that if you aim at nothing, you'll probably hit it. If you don't want to get anywhere, any road will do. If you want to change your life without working, you'll have to find a magician. But I believe that if you stick with me, you will see results almost immediately. I believe that you will love the results you see, and I hope you will enjoy the process.

Whoever you are and whatever you want, I know that you are capable of achieving it. In fact, I know that you are capable of achieving much more. I have met thousands of people, from drug addicts to the chairmen of large corporations, and they all have one thing in common: each one is a remarkable person. We all have the basic tools and abilities to achieve remarkable things. We simply have to learn to use them. When you've done that, you'll be ready to enjoy the Contract for Utmost Living, which you'll find at the end of the book, and transform your life.

1

. . .

Finding a Place for
Your Dreams

My hometown diner is a classic, with double-wing steps leading
up to an entryway ornamented with arcade games, an aquamarine and
silver starburst façade, booths upholstered in oxblood, a counter along
one side, and sunshine spilling all over everywhere. Anyone who comes
in here for breakfast can't help feeling they've made a good start on the
day.

I come here once or twice a week when I'm in town, but I'm not a
real regular like Larry King, two booths down. He's here nearly every
day that he's not taping his show in New York, usually with three
friends. I bet more of the world's problems get solved at that table than
at cabinet meetings—solved at least long enough for them to finish
their eggs, that is. Steven Spielberg drops in fairly often, looking like
he's thinking about the world that's inside his head.

I don't need to tell you I enjoy seeing these people, sitting in
the same diner they sit in, just like I belong there. Me, a kid from a

lower-income family in Whittier, California. *Is this cool or what?* I'm thinking. I mean, I've spoken all over the world, I've addressed the U.S. Congress, I've met stars in all sorts of fields, and I'm still just tickled by the whole thing. By life. You wouldn't believe it.

Unless, of course, you believe that anything is possible. And that's what I'm here to tell you. Anything you can think of can become real. In fact, it will become real—that's the law of attraction. Anything is possible. It really is. Go ahead, say it to yourself. Say it out loud. Say it like you mean it, because before you finish reading this book, you are going to mean it. You are going to mean it about yourself and you are going to live it. Anything is possible. And it will feel great.

Life Is Yours for the Taking

I am the number one fan of the Anything Is Possible Network—APN for short. One time I was watching football with a friend of mine who lives out in the country. Way out. And like me, he is a big football fan, so he was really excited about his new satellite dish and what it could do for him. "Tim, watch this," he said. "Wherever I shift the dish, that's what I pick up. I can watch games on the East Coast, in the Midwest, or anywhere." Listen to that again: "Wherever I shift the dish, that's what I pick up." We need to have a dish like that in our hearts and in our heads. Because you could be picking up the I'm So Stupid Network or the It's Too Hard Network or any one of hundreds of other networks that are going to get you down when you pick them up. When you tune in to APN, you are going to pick up something that is going to pick you up.

One of my most interesting friends is Duane Chapman, better known as Dog the Bounty Hunter. I was introduced to him many years ago, when he was a bounty hunter, but before he became famous and made famous mistakes. He was working in Hawaii and in Denver, but he wasn't happy. He knew there was more to life than what he had then. With Beth, his common-law wife, Dog and I began to spend quality time together. I talked to them a little about corners in life. A corner is a bend or a curve that you can't see around. Sometimes your life just seems like it's moving in a straight line—you're ordering up the same thing every day, every week, every month. But if you shift your dish, you will come to a corner, and you never know what wonderful things may lie around that corner.

Dog had faith, and he turned that corner. Just around the corner he was offered a show with A&E, which is now that channel's most popular one. And then his autobiography became a number one bestseller. I was at his wedding to Beth—after living together for sixteen years they finally decided to get married—and we were out on the ocean in an outrigger canoe. The A&E people were there, celebrities were there, and hundreds of people were lined up on the rocks on the shore, cheering for Dog and yelling congratulations. Dog began to cry. "Can you imagine this?" he said through the tears. "Look how far God has brought me." If you shift your dish, good things are waiting just around the corner.

When I go to my diner, I can sometimes tell which of the people there do not believe that anything is possible. The people I worry about are the ones sitting alone at those tables near the kitchen. There's Jack right now. He's always there, pretending to read the paper while he's eavesdropping on the conversations around him. Always next to the kitchen door, which isn't exactly Siberia—the diner's not that big—but surely isn't Venice Beach. It's noisy, the waiters are always rushing by, there are the steam and smells and heat of the kitchen. I tip my Dodgers cap to him and he nods back. Jack's not a bad-looking guy, if you don't mind a little piercing. Dark hair and about as pale as you can get in Los Angeles.

Frances comes by. "Where ya wanna be today, Tim? By the window? Are ya gonna flip a coin?" Frances is always a reality check for me. She doesn't assume anything, so she makes me think about making a choice. Even about where I sit. Today I've decided I have a job to do.

As it turns out, now is the moment you've been waiting for.

—Lucinda Williams

"I'll just sit over there today, Frances, thanks."

"There? By the kitchen? You wanna know what Lou's making for the special today?"

"Just for a change, Frances. Humor me."

"That's me, the Good Humor girl. Juice?"

"That's me. I'll just take a look at the menu."

"Suit yourself. It's not like it's changed since Tuesday."

"Maybe I have." I take a seat and look over at Jack, who's pretending not to look over at me, even though he knows I'm usually across the room. I lean over to him. "Excuse me, is that today's *Times*?"

"Yeah," he says, and he thinks about whether to take the next step. He does. "But I wouldn't say the news is all that fresh."

I laugh with him. Jack's willingness to strike up a conversation tells me he's open for a change, or at least an exchange. Jack's already made a choice, and I already feel like the day's going to be a good one. I can help people who don't acknowledge that they need help, but it's a lot easier when they do.

Live by Design, Not by Default

I've talked to a lot of people like Jack. Jack himself doesn't know why he always sits near the kitchen—it's just where he landed the first time he came to the diner and he's never sat anywhere else. Jack is living by default, not by design. For him, whatever was has become what is and what will be. Jack has not tuned in to APN.

You might think there's nothing really wrong with just letting small, bothersome things be. Small, bothersome, distressing, distorting, depressing things. Maybe if it's only for this morning, I could let that go. You can't change everything all at once. I could even let it go if it's only for today. But to live a life full of small, bothersome, distressing, distorting, depressing things is a default life. It is a life full of static that keeps you from tuning in to the Anything Is Possible Network, which is broadcasting in powerful high-definition 24/7. You're getting the static, not the signal. You are trying to skip with your shoelaces tied together; you are trying to sing with a gag in your mouth; you are trying to make art with a blindfold on. Remember: your life is a joy, it is your song, it is your masterpiece.

> *Success is not the result of spontaneous combustion. You must set yourself on fire.*
>
> —Fred Shero

It's time to untie the laces, throw away the gag, and stuff that blindfold in the trash. You are here to do something divinely wonderful. Why else would God put you on earth? He doesn't do things halfway.

He doesn't say to Himself, "Well, I think I'll just create a little, not-very-important human being today. Just try one out, you know. See how it goes. Maybe tomorrow I'll work a little harder." He gives you everything He's got and He wants you to use it. Why else go through all this?

I am going to help you find your way to the best life you can have, to your utmost life. I'm going to give you the tools to order up the life you want, and I'm going to help you discover what that life is and what is keeping you from living it.

I'm looking at the menu when suddenly there's a bellow from the kitchen that startles Jack and me both. "Pick up! Let's go! Diligent hands bring wealth!" I have to smile; one of the reasons I like this place is that the owner can quote Solomon. It takes me a few minutes to order, but Jack just says, "The usual," without looking at the menu. I ask him if he likes the food here.

"Oh, it's OK, I guess." I raise my eyebrows, look at him some more. "Well, actually, it's pretty bad."

"Oh, I'm sorry you don't like it. Do you always order the same thing?" We strike up a conversation, and Jack asks me what I do. When I tell him that I'm a life coach, he looks a little startled and says, "Boy, that must be awesome. But I could never do it. Sometimes I'm not even sure what sport I'm playing."

Sitting at the same table is not the only part of his life Jack just accepts. He always orders the same thing because it's too hard for him to decide about something different every morning. He doesn't complain when the food is bad, because he comes here nearly every day and he doesn't want them getting mad at him. He doesn't go to another diner because the food might be even worse. For Jack, there are obstacles at every turn.

Jack is living a life by default. Jack has become a victim—a victim of circumstances. Don't let that happen to you. You have options; you can do something different. Wake yourself up and take a look around at the environment you've made for yourself. Don't keep swallowing things that make you sick. You can change the faces, the places, and the spaces in your world. Circumstances don't have you, you have them. Stop being a victim *of* circumstances and start being a victor *over* circumstances.

Don't Let Your Past Predict Your Present

The kinds of things that are holding Jack back are just the tip of the iceberg. I've seen that myself. We were not a wealthy family. In fact, we were a poor family. In fact, we were po' folk, but my parents made our lives rich. We were a happy family. I loved sports, and as long as I could play, I was fine. There's a picture of me in my Little League uniform: skinny, big smile, big Afro with my Little League cap perched on top of it. And there's this big rip in my jeans. I didn't care; my family didn't care about things like that. It's like we didn't know we were poor, so it didn't matter. My mother worked hard, and if we were always close to not making it, she kept us in Special K, which she'd buy in bulk. You'd look in our kitchen cabinets and there'd be nothing but Special K.

My parents didn't have much money to spend, but they had lots of love that they spent on us, and we were happy. My father loved to spend time with us. He'd say, "We're going on a family drive," and we would all pile into the station wagon. Some of my best memories were when all seven of us were packed into our station wagon for family trips. Once we drove all the way from Los Angeles to Seattle, and I still don't know how five little kids survived in that tiny space for such a long time. If it hadn't been for Mom and Dad's great sense of humor, I think we kids could have done some serious damage to one another. But my parents always had us laughing.

I remember especially one time we all drove to Big Bear Mountain, which is a recreation park in southern California. We began to talk about what we would like to accomplish. We began to dream; we began to think big in that small space.

Then when we drove up, there were all these people skiing. I had never seen anyone ski before, not in person. Somebody in the car said, "People like us don't ski." That didn't seem right to me then, and it doesn't seem right to me now. You can do anything you want, you can be anything you want. Anything is possible.

Dad loved his family and wanted each of us kids to reach our full potential. Then one day a police officer showed up at our front door. As I listened to the officer tell Mom that Dad had been in an accident and wouldn't be coming home, I felt that the wonderful life I had enjoyed for eleven years was over. That night I heard Mom wailing in her bedroom. I had never heard anyone cry that way before, nor have I ever heard anything like it since.

I was keenly aware that I was living in a bad dream. Someone had dished up a meal for me that I didn't want to swallow, and for months and months it was as if I had a stomachache every minute. But no matter how much I tried, I couldn't spit it out, couldn't send it back, couldn't get rid of the awful taste in my mouth that came from the news of my dad's death. I didn't know what to do. My mother had to work all the time to keep us alive. She worked in Winchell's, a donut shop, and sometimes she would be working two shifts a day, and she would come home exhausted.

All the rest of us had to find new ways to live a life that had the biggest hole in the world in it. I watched my sisters and my brother find their own ways to live, their own ways to soothe the pain or deaden it. My oldest sister did her best with the rest of us. My other sisters focused their attention on school or jobs. My brother tried to numb himself with alcohol, as he had watched other people do.

Two years after my father died, my sister Viola was in a car accident and fell into a coma. We all came to her bedside and watched over her, prayed for her, but she never regained consciousness. I was old enough to hurt and young enough to find it difficult to express my grief. I wanted to scream, "Hey, I didn't order this. I don't want to listen to my mother cry in her room at night. I can't stand this pain. I want my father and my sister back." At that early age, I began trying to make sense of the senselessness around me, and I had a deep desire within me to fix everyone else's pain. I knew there had to be a better reality than the one I was facing. I envisioned that reality, and it has come true.

Excuses Are a Starvation Diet

I probably have my mother to thank for making me take responsibility for finding that better reality. She wouldn't let me make excuses for myself. She tried to teach me there was more to life than sports and dancing. She made me scrub the floors at Winchell's after her late shift. She said to me, "Don't do half a job." I learned the discipline of doing things all the way, no matter what challenges presented themselves.

Whatever we want to do, there are almost always obstacles we have to overcome. They may be external, such as a lack of money or physically being in the wrong place. You can't train horses in Antarctica. If you're seven foot two, you're not going to be a jockey. You may have family responsibilities that you can't shirk. You may need to learn a new skill, reach out to new people, or otherwise change the way you live your life. The obstacles may be internal—old habits, old rules that have been passed down, a lack of self-confidence, fear.

Whatever they are, they're not adding to your life, they are adding to your drag. You're dragging around all this extra weight. You're not who you really are, you're that person plus all that other weight. In the years after my father died, I carried around a lot of weight. I wasn't doing well in school, my father was gone, and my family was searching for a center. It was a long time before things started to get better.

If you don't get out of the box you were raised in, you won't understand how much bigger the world is.

—Angelina Jolie

I had difficulty with reading and writing, so I was labeled a "troubled student." That was the label they put on me, even when they didn't say those words to my face. That label determined how I was looked at, how people treated me, and even how I felt about myself. That label became my image. The dictionary defines *image* as "the opinion or concept of something that is held by the public," or "the character projected to the public." I picked up that label, put it on my forehead, and wore it all over that school. I was the class clown, I didn't pay attention in school, I didn't make any efforts with my schoolwork.

I had to find out how to get beyond this world of setbacks, to tear off those labels. And I did, but I didn't do it alone. It happened because of some things I chose, and it happened because of some things that chose me. One of the things that chose me was Mr. Probert.

Mr. Probert was one of my teachers, and a funny guy. He looked and acted a little like Mr. Rogers. Even down to the sweaters. He'd come into class, take his sweater off, fold it up, and put it in a plastic bag, like he was working at Brooks Brothers. But he wouldn't accept my label. He told me I should work harder, because I was better than I thought. He saw the best in me, not the label on me. He argued with me a lot, and in the end he won. He convinced me that I had value. Mr. Probert saved my soul.

I realize now that Mr. Probert saw me from a God's-eye view. I don't know if he would say it that way, and you don't have to say it that way, but you can see it that way no matter how you say it. I didn't have to show Mr. Probert anything. I didn't have to turn somersaults, do math problems, or show him my Superman suit. He just knew it was there.

I'm not free until I believe in me.

—Robert H. Schuller

And I've learned that it's there in everyone. Some of you may think that doing something wonderful is beyond you. You're too young, you're too poor, you're too dumb, you're too shy. And all those may be true all at once. That doesn't mean you aren't a wonder.

Remember, there are many kinds of wonderful. Some kinds are obvious, but not all of them. Maybe not even most of them. Before you can see what your life's purpose is, you need to clear away the things that are obscuring your vision, diverting you from your true path, and dulling your appetite for life without really nourishing you. It's time to take a look around, rub that sleep out of your eyes, and ask yourself, *Is this what I want to be doing? Is this what I want to be doing? Is this what I want to be doing?*

Take some time to inventory your personal pantry. What are the things about yourself that you can't change? What are the things about you that you absolutely wouldn't change even if you could? What are your strengths? If you have trouble making that decision, what are the things that other people say are your strengths? We're putting together a list of ingredients for your success, and once we have the things that are givens in your life, we're going to look for the gift—your true hunger, the strength that will make you a world shaker and a history maker.

Charles Schwab, the fantastically successful investment counselor, also had trouble in school when he was a child. He could do well in science and math, but anything that involved reading and writing were really difficult. But he didn't let his problems bring him down, didn't let them become excuses for himself; he just kept doing his best. And you can see that his best was pretty spectacular.

Years later, when his son was diagnosed with dyslexia, he realized that he had had the same problem all the time. But he thinks that his disability actually worked to his advantage. "I worked harder to overcompensate," he says. "My SAT scores were pretty bad, but my enthusiasm, commitment, and hard work were impressive. And because I had to work harder than the other kids, I had self-confidence."

Once you say you're going to settle for second, that's what happens to you in life.

—John F. Kennedy

We all have challenges in our lives; we're all good at some things and not so good at others. Life will deal us some bad breaks, hard shakes, and heartaches. Whatever they are in your life, don't let them keep you from the real work, the real worth of your life. Don't let yourself have an "almost" life. You know, "I almost made the team" or "I almost got the job." And don't even let yourself settle for a "mostly" life—"I'm mostly happy" or "My life is mostly OK." No. Take your life to the utmost.

Take responsibility for your life and for making your life the utmost it can be. I'll show you how.

Make Your Own Menu

When you sit down to order a meal, you first decide—probably without even thinking about it—what you *don't* want to eat. If you're there at 9:00 A.M., you probably skip the roast beef dinner. If it's dinnertime, you probably won't be satisfied with tea and toast. But that decision has to be what you want, and what will give you the energy you need. If you've been working hard since four in the morning, you'll want something hearty. Just don't be like Jack, who didn't even really order. If you keep doing things as you've always done them, what you'll get is what you've already got.

At the end of this chapter and of each chapter of this book, you'll find guides and questions that will help you get started writing your own menu for the life you're truly destined to live. Now, I'm sure that some of you out there just decided—unconsciously—that you're not going to read any farther. Suddenly this has started to seem like work. Oh, you'll run your eyes down the pages, but reading this book is not about letting it go in one eye and out the other. Maybe you've consciously decided it. Or maybe you haven't really decided anything, but in fact you've picked up twenty books like this and always stopped just when you have to play an active part in your own renovation. Well, give me five minutes.

That's all I'm saying, five minutes. Is that a long time? Just stop for five minutes and dream with me. We're going to have a wonderful dream together, and it's going to be about you. Dream about feeling that you have an abundance of life all around you and in you. You are doing work that satisfies you, stretches you, and fulfills you. You wake up in the morning with an excitement in you—you're already planning how you are going to spend the day, because it's just a joy to think about.

You have a glide in your stride and a skip in your step all day because you have satisfaction, you have rewards, you have work that is good for you. Maybe it's because of money, or maybe it's because of love, but more likely those things are what happens after you have started living your utmost life.

I don't know about you, but I am convinced that you can have that dream—if you are willing to do the work. Attracting the life you want by thinking the right thoughts might sound easy, but it won't happen unless you make it happen. And I believe that you will start to see a difference almost immediately—if you are willing to do the work. Some of it will be hard, but most of it will be absorbing. After all, it's all about you.

> *To work—to work! It is such infinite delight to know that we still have the best things to do.*
>
> —Katherine Mansfield

I'm going to make it easy on you at the start—all you have to do is complain. That is, you may find it easier to make a list of what you don't want before you can clearly see your heart's desires. To help bring your core desires into focus, make a list of what you don't want to swallow anymore. Finish the sentence: *I don't want . . .*

I don't want to be fat.

I don't want to wake up feeling like I don't want to get out of bed.

I don't want to feel the rest of the world is enjoying what I don't have.

I don't want to work at this job I don't care about.

I don't want to always be denying myself things and experiences just because I don't have the time.

I don't want to be too out of shape to enjoy playing ball with my kids.

I don't want to meet men only in bars.

I don't want to argue with my wife every time we talk about money.

Maybe you need some examples before you start your list. It's surprising that sometimes when we start to actually write down what's bothering us, the things we think of don't seem so important all of a sudden. But they are.

Think about what you did yesterday. Think about the whole day, from start to finish, or think about today as you live it. That's always a good thing to do, and remember that you're actually *living*—you're not just sitting on a shelf, you're not freeze-dried, your life doesn't need to be microwaved to get it going. You remember the old joke "This can't be my real life, because if it were, there would be a user's manual"? Well, we're making up that user's manual as we go along.

So think about your day, yesterday or even today. Write down the things that happened that you didn't like. It could be something you did, or somewhere you went, or even just something you felt. Maybe you didn't call that friend you said you'd call back. Maybe you got mad at your neighbor because she lets her cats use your yard as their litter box. Maybe you were bored at your job. Maybe you didn't spend time with your kids because you were tired. Maybe you ate too much or drank too much. Maybe you didn't write down the things you didn't like.

Which one, or which ones, of them have bugged you for a long time? Are there any of them that you can change? Can you go over and talk to that neighbor? Can you eat one less Twinkie or have one less drink? Can you take your lunch hour and get out of your office to do something fun and different? Maybe just for one day. When I say change, I just mean *change*—I don't mean *transform* or *erase* or *obliterate*. Just give it a little twist, open up a window, crank it up or down a notch. See what happens.

> *If you don't do something with life,*
> *life will do something with you.*

What I'm saying is that I want you to look for ways you can take control of your life. I want you to begin to see and feel and taste that you can be in control of your life. You can start with small things and see how it goes, because you're going to get there—you're going to get to a place where you can control your destiny. You can change the places, spaces, and faces that are in your life. And if they're in your way, if they are keeping you from living a full life, then you need to.

Now we'll do something that may be even more important. For the things in your life that you can't change, write down why you can't. The reasons may be outside you, or they may be inside you. Or maybe you can't tell exactly *why* you can't change something; you just think or know or fear that you can't. We'll get back to those. In fact, nothing you do for this book, which is really for yourself, is wasted.

Now, I've tried this, and I know that it can get a little depressing just to think about all the things you don't like about your life, even when they're not your fault. More important, saying what you *don't* want with your life doesn't get you any further along the road to what you *do* want. So while you were writing down the things you didn't like about your day, you might have thought of some things you really did like. That's great. Write those down as well, and put a box around them and add a little star or two. As you write down the things you don't want, the things you do want will become ever more clear to you. Try reversing the previous list to see if your core desires are now more obvious to you. Your list may now read:

I want to look good.

I want to work at a job that satisfies me.

I want to have time to see friends and learn new things.

I want to be financially secure so that I can provide what my family and I need and like.

I want to exercise more.

I want to buy a boat.

I want to be able to tell my wife what I think.

Now pick one of those wants—maybe not the most important one—to begin with. Ask yourself if you're willing to change your life in order to make it come true. When you answer yes to one of them, circle it. We'll come back to that too.

The more you think about your life, about what makes you content or satisfied or gratified, the more you will think about the larger purpose and meaning of your life. I've spent a lot of time thinking about these things and helping other people to think about them. I've found that I want to live by design to my God-given purpose; I want to fulfill my purpose for being on earth.

To Jack, I suggest that he might enjoy his meal a little better if he sat nearer the window, in the sunshine. Jack's breakfast arrives. The eggs are runny and the toast burned, but Jack doesn't act like he notices. I call over Frances and point to Jack's toast and eggs. "Frances," I say, "is that what you would serve your boys?"

"Hey," she shoots back, "that's the way he's always had his eggs and toast. We thought he liked them that way." Jack looks sheepishly at me while Frances heads for the kitchen.

I hope Jack sees that he can refuse to accept whatever he's served without being a whiner or a complainer. You have options, and it's your God-given right to become awake to them and aware of your environment before you make the choices that will lead you to the place you want to be. There was no reason for Jack to be a victim—to keep on sitting somewhere unpleasant and eating food he didn't like—but until he makes a statement and takes a stand, he'll never know what his purpose is. Take a moment every day to look at the places, spaces, and faces in your life and ask yourself if they are the ones you want there. Make some new choices tomorrow, even just in small matters. Think of something you can do differently right now, or at least by tomorrow—some simple thing that changes your routine. You'll be surprised at how even a small change can birth a new idea in you. Soon you'll gain the confidence to make bigger decisions in more important areas of your life.

- Your destiny is a matter of choice in the present, not the chance of your past.
- Excuses definitely won't get you what you want.
- Try to change something in your life today.

Getting Down to Business

YOUR UTMOST LIVING JOURNAL

This section at the end of each chapter will give you some specific suggestions about discovering where you want to go with your life and planning how to get there. We'll begin by taking stock. Think about yourself—the characteristics of yourself that you can't change and the ones that you absolutely wouldn't change even if you could. What would change and how? Start thinking about the person you want to be.

	TODAY	EVENTUALLY
Income		
Career		
Friendships		
Intimate relationships		
Appearance		
Health		
Exercise		
Leisure time		
Education		
Skills		

The various aspects of our lives all present different ways to grow and change. You may already know the area of your life that you want to work on, but if you don't or if you can't decide, here are some ideas to get you started. I've listed a few characteristics that are often mentioned when people talk about what they want to change in their lives. As we said in the first chapter, it may be easiest for you to start thinking about what you don't want in your life, but as we've learned, it's most effective when you then think of these things in positive terms. I've offered some of the "don't wants," and left you to fill in other "do wants."

As you think about translating your "don't wants" into your "do wants," remember to look for an opposite that is both right for you and possible for your situation. The opposite of "fat" is not "bony"; it's the right weight for your body type. The opposite of "angry" is not always "at peace"; for you it might mean action—using that anger to change your life in a good way.

Think of this step as planning the menu for your life. You won't do everything at once, just as you wouldn't eat salad, pasta, steak, and ice cream on the same plate. But this will help you decide what your most satisfying life will be composed of.

Physically

I DON'T WANT TO BE . . .	I WANT TO BE . . .
Fat	Fit
Sick	Healthy
Tired	
Unattractive	

Personally

I DON'T WANT TO BE . . .	I WANT TO BE . . .
Lonely	In a fulfilling relationship
Bored	Engaged
Angry	
Worried	

Socially

I DON'T WANT TO BE . . .
Isolated
Dominated by others
Lost in the crowd

I WANT TO . . .
Have close friends
Be in control of my time
with others

Professionally

I DON'T WANT . . .
To be stuck in my current job
To be a follower
To worry about money

I WANT . . .
A new job
To be part of a great team

Spiritually

I DON'T WANT TO . . .
Feel that I have to do everything
with my own strength
Live in a cold, merciless world

I WANT TO . . .
Feel that there is
a purpose to life
Feel a part of a greater whole

2

. . .

What Makes You Hungry?

We always know when we're hungry, but we don't always know what we're hungry *for.* The same is true in our lives—we know that we want to do more, to see more, to be more—but we're not always sure exactly how to gratify those hungers.

According to the dictionary, appetite is "an instinctive physical urge." Hunger is so basic that it's part of our physical makeup. It's the mountaintop you want to reach, the door you want to open, the fire you want to light. True hunger is the lack of some nutrient, some essential element that allows you to grow. Satisfying that hunger is about satisfying your spirit, allowing it to grow. That hunger comes from a God idea.

There's a difference between a good idea and a God idea. Good ideas are good things, usually. They make your life a little better, a little easier, or a little happier, maybe all three. Good ideas spring from what is happening in your daily life, and you need all of them you can birth, beg, or borrow. Just making it out of bed in the morning and getting all the way back into bed at night can be an exhausting journey.

Our lives are so busy that it's easy to forget our dreams. But we never lose our appetite, so even when we haven't found that God idea, we try to satisfy that hunger with something else. Like working too much. Or playing too much. Or depending too much on someone else for our happiness. Or watching TV too much. We get filled up every day with the spiritual equivalent of junk food—somebody's temper tantrum at work, a disappointment about something that seemed to be an opportunity, being ignored by someone we love.

> *No man is born into the world whose work is not born with him.*
>
> —James Russell Lowell

We become filled up until we can't take any more, but we're not really satisfied. You know that feeling you have after getting a big ol' bag of take-out food—too much bread, too many fries and chips and cheese, too much sweet soda and ice cream. Oof. You're just melding with the couch, right? Can't move a muscle. That's what it feels like to live without a God idea. You can't move.

Don't Let Other People Choose for You

The next time I go to my diner, it's for lunch—a friend has invited me. Lunch at the diner has a different feeling than breakfast does—people are distracted by their jobs or errands, and they are often just squeezing in a meal before they go back to their responsibilities. My friend is no exception. "This menu," she says. "How can I ever choose? What are you going to have, Tim?"

"I'm still looking. You just go ahead."

"You must have a thousand meals here," Selene says to the waitress. "I'll just have this one," she says, pointing at the menu.

"Ya mean the Judy Garland, honey?"

Selene rolls her eyes and nods. Hey, it's L.A.

"You like the salads here?" I ask.

"Oh, they're OK, I guess." Selene shrugs. "But I mean really, if they would just organize the menu a little better . . . They list every salad separately. They should have the main ingredients on one side and the things you can add to them on the other and let you choose. I'm not really that hungry. My sister was telling me yesterday that I really needed to lose some weight. Do you think I'm fat, Tim?"

"I think you're fabulous. If you're not hungry, then why are you eating?"

"Well, I wanted to talk to you, and lunch is really the only time I can get away from my job. My boss is always telling me that I would do better if I worked more. But at least he thinks people should eat. He thinks I'm too thin. Do you think I'm too thin? Mark says I should just eat more protein and stop worrying about my job."

"Whoa there," I say. "You're telling me that you're not hungry for food, you're hungry for talk."

There's no sauce in the world
like hunger.

—Miguel de Cervantes

Too often, we just get through life. We get a job, we get a boyfriend or girlfriend, we get a hobby. It fills us up, but in the end it doesn't satisfy. And we even feel guilty that it doesn't satisfy us, because everything around us is telling us what's important. It's important to have a sleek car or a big house. It's important to have lots of friends; it's important to be in charge; it's important to have washboard abs or a tight butt. But in fact, we don't really care about a lot of those things—we don't really want to spend the money, do the workouts, meet the people, or learn the skills. We wind up feeling guilty about not having something we never really wanted in the first place.

Unlike Jack, Selene is the kind of person who does think about what she is doing—but usually lets other people's needs and desires make the decision for her. You need to realize that you should be feeding your hunger—your real hunger, not what someone else or society dictates. No one else can understand and fulfill your life's purpose, whatever it is.

> *Motivation is a fire from within. If someone else tries to light that fire under you, chances are it will burn very briefly.*
>
> —Stephen Covey

Selene's life isn't satisfying to her. She isn't exactly unhappy, but she isn't really getting any lift from her life. She was thinking about going to a doctor for antidepressants. I ask her if her job is what she would like it to be. "Mostly," she answers. "It's a job, you know. I like design, and the computers make it easy, and my boss says if I stay around long enough something will open up. It's just no fun waiting."

"And what about the rest of your life? Is that the way you want it?"

"Almost. I mean, Mark's nice, he really is. He'd be especially nice if he proposed, but he says there's no reason to rush into it. And it's not like I have that much to do after work. Mark works late a lot, but he likes for me to be home when he gets home. So I have lots of free time."

"Sounds to me like that's your problem."

"Is that one of your parables? What do you mean?"

"You're not feeding your hunger. I think maybe I have to tell you about when I was a teenager."

"Tim, I'm thirty-two years old."

"Really?"

"Timmm . . ."

"All right, all right, but all I know is what I've got. I was a skinny kid, but I was a good athlete. Picture that: big Afro, Converse high-tops. From the time I was about ten until I was about fourteen, I ruled. There were two other guys I competed with, and we were the best. But then, once we hit fourteen, they started to pull away from me. Suddenly I wasn't one of the top three athletes in the school anymore. That really messed me up. I lost the thing that defined me. But what I discovered was that I was letting other people define me. I was using the abilities I had, and doing things I liked, but it turns out I only liked them if I was the best. If I wasn't coming in first, I felt like I was a nobody.

> *The whole secret of a successful life is*
> *to find out what it is one's destiny to*
> *do, and then do it.*
>
> —Henry Ford

"It took me years to shake off these feelings that if I wasn't first, I wasn't anything at all. And even longer to stop looking outside myself for satisfaction, for the standards of judgment, for the goals I wanted to achieve. Ultimately, I learned that the things I needed to know, the real goals that I needed to achieve, were inside me."

After that I let Selene talk, but she had understood what I hope you'll understand: everyone comes to life with a promise. You can think of it as a promise from God, as I do, or you can think of it as a promise wrapped up inside you—a promise you've been given or a promise you have. The dictionary defines *promise* as "a statement of what you will or will not do" or "a basis for expectation." Both of them are true about us. The promise we have is our basis for expecting our lives to be great—and we must make a statement that we will make that promise come to pass.

Selene hasn't discovered—hasn't taken the time to find—what her promise is, what her purpose is. She could be taking classes, meeting people who are doing what she wants to be doing, or even just reading about something that excites her. But the first thing for her to do is to discover for herself what she wants. You have to be absolutely clear about what it is you want. Only Selene can discover what essential nutrient she's missing so that she can satisfy that hunger and become not only what *she* hungers to be but also what she *hungers* to be. Because otherwise she'll be right back in the same place.

The 3 Ps: Purpose, Passions, and Priorities

There are some things you need to know about yourself, and they are not necessarily obvious to you. Of course, you should take inventory of the things that are obvious and that you can't change, such as your height and your age, but they are not what will chart your course. You have to know the 3 Ps: your purpose, your passions, and your priorities.

First, there's your **purpose.** Your purpose is the reason that you do everything else. It's the fundamental idea that moves your soul. That's a big thing, and it may take you a while to know it. It's about leaving some kind of mark. There's a wonderful story about a group of Catholic nuns who are traveling the United States in a bus. Their parishioners have scraped together enough money to send the whole convent on a monthlong tour of the Great Southwest. The nuns start out from Wisconsin and head south into Texas, then west into Arizona. They are awed by the Painted Desert and the Grand Canyon, impressed by Hoover Dam. At every stop, one of them, Sister Clara, gets out of the bus, walks around a bit, then picks up a stone and moves it. Sometimes it's a really big stone. The rest of the group tolerate this peculiarity, but naturally they are curious.

Halfway through the trip, they hit Death Valley, and sure enough, when the bus stops, Sister Clara gets out and starts looking around. This time she picks up a really big stone, a real rock, and when she finally heaves it out of the ground, she goes head over heels into the dust. The nuns rush to see if she's all right. She's fine and they all return to the bus.

In the bus, one of the nuns turns to Sister Clara and says that they are all concerned for her safety. And finally, she asks the question they've all been wanting to ask: "Why do you always move a stone when we stop?" Understanding their concern, Sister Clara answers, "I turn a stone so that the place is different because I have been there."

Here our duty is to become more ourselves, not less.

—Thomas Merton

Your purpose is what you want to do so that this place will be different because you've been here. It could be as big as running a company or running the marathon in the Olympics. It could be as small as raising children who know and care about their world and what they can do for it. No, that's not small. It could be assembling the biggest and best collection of baseball trading cups from 7-Eleven. I've got about three hundred to help you get started. You'll think that's funny; "Tim," you say, "how important is collecting baseball trading cups?" The thing is, though, that I know once you've accumulated that knock-your-socks-off-collection-to-end-all-collections, you'll want that feeling of accomplishment again. And you'll want to do something that's even better.

So stop and think about what you would like to do that will make a difference in this world. Purpose is your reason for living, the force within you that gives you the desire to act. Life without a purpose is just an experiment.

Some people are lucky; they know their purpose as if from the moment they're born. Barbra Streisand knew she wanted to sing; Michael Jordan knew he wanted to use his athletic gifts. They knew that was how they would leave their mark on the world. But there's a difference between a gift that guides and a need that drives. A purpose is not an obsession or an addiction.

A Life That's Valuable Is a Life with Values

Values are crucial to your life's purpose. Value is about worth, and if you don't have values, your life isn't worth much. We spend too much time worrying about what something costs without taking into account what it's worth. Nothing in life is separate from anything else, no matter how convenient it would be to think so.

Suppose someone decides to give a lot of money to charities—

worthy causes, as we say—but he makes that money by selling drugs. The value of the money he gives to charity is wiped out by the lives he has destroyed with drugs. Suppose someone works sixteen hours a day at two different organizations that feed and clothe the homeless, but spends all the money he earns drinking. The value of his good work is leveled by the destruction of his own life. Some people will fight for power at the expense of anyone and everyone who stands in their way. I suspect such people aren't reading this book—but maybe they will if they realize that winning at someone else's expense is a diet that eventually sickens you.

Labor to keep alive in your breast that little spark of celestial fire called conscience.

—George Washington

But many of us may have to take some time to consider what our purpose is. We have been so swamped with people telling us what to do that it may take us a while to know our own heart's purpose. I'm sure you can write down all those things that the candidates for Miss America used to say to Bert Parks: "I want to help disadvantaged people," "I want to make the world a better place to live in," "I want to heal the sick," and so forth. These are all worthy purposes, and I'm sure that each and every one of the Miss America hopefuls went on to fulfill them once they stepped off the runway.

But your life's purpose may not be so grand, and I hope it's not so general. You may want to lift people's spirits, and do it by playing the guitar. You may want to make your family's life safe and comfortable, which means you need to earn enough money. You may want to distinguish yourself from everyone else by collecting all those trading cups—but I hope you'll donate them to a good cause when you're done.

---

*Don't be too big to do
something small.*

—Max Lucado

You can keep on working to refine that purpose as well. *How* do you want to heal the sick? *How* do you want to make the world a better place to live in? If your purpose is to make our society work better, you might not be able to run for national office, but you can run for the school board, coach the Little League team, or work with the PTA. If your purpose is to heal the sick, you may not develop a groundbreaking vaccine, but you can work to make sick people's lives easier or a lonely child's world brighter.

The Energy Source: Your Passions in Life

Once you know what your purpose is, you may find yourself thinking about the next step: your **passions.** Passions are the energy food—one of the things that keep us going, that give us the get-up-and-go, the oomph to stick to the job even when it's difficult, when we're discouraged, when we're down.

"Oh, Tim, come on," Selene says. "I know that. And I like my job. I'm not complaining about going to work. And I really have fun with Mark."

"But?"

"Well, yeah. What do you think I should do?"

"We're not talking about me here. We're talking about you."

"No fair, I asked you first. Anyway, I'm exhausted. I was up all night working on a redesign of a film poster that my boss screwed up."

"That come out OK?"

"It's a killer, but he'll never say that. *And* he'll tell everyone that he did it."

Selene talks to me for another half an hour about her poster, and I point out to her that for someone who's exhausted, she has more life coming out of her eyes than anyone else in the room. I can find your passion by what comes out of your mouth. It's the thing that stirs you up. I was talking to someone the other day whose passion was plants. He couldn't be stopped—he told me about winter plants and summer plants and how long the winter plants could last and when you should plant the summer plants and when they would flower and how much fertilizer and water and . . . you get the idea.

Once when I went to hear Stevie Wonder sing, he said, "Now you've entered into my world." For two hours I was enveloped in this man's passion. Stevie Wonder has put them together—his passion is his purpose—and you can do that too. That's where we're going here. I want you to get to a point in your life where you so enjoy what you're doing that people can draw from it.

Think back to the last time you felt yourself so deeply involved in a conversation that you didn't want to stop talking. Maybe it was about the state of the Union, or baseball, or the weather. I know that every once in a while I'll take a minute to look up something or write something down, and I'll find that I just can't stop. Even though I have an appointment or someone is waiting for me to send them something, I'm just so caught up, so lifted up by what I'm doing, that I can't stop myself. Why not spend your whole life feeling like that?

I was the class clown until Mr. Probert made me respect myself, but

·I would have been foolish to ignore the fact that I loved comedy, and I loved to perform. I used to listen to Bill Cosby tapes and memorize them, and then the next day I'd do the whole routine for my friends in school—until the teacher would pull me by the ear and make me sit outside. I also loved helping people. If there was a kid at school everybody made fun of, I'd take his side. If he didn't have money for lunch, I'd loan him money. I eventually put together those things that are the real me and here I am, a minister and a motivational speaker.

Bob Newhart, the comedian, is a perfect example of someone whose passion ultimately made him give up the job that society said he should have, and create the one that his passion demanded. Although he loved to listen to comedians when he was a kid, he felt that he had to go to school and learn something that would be dependable and safe. So he graduated from college with a degree in accounting. But he never felt comfortable being an accountant. If the petty cash drawer came up short, he would just put some of his own money in to make it come out even.

When he was bored, he would call up a friend and make up elaborate funny stories. In fact, the stories were so funny that one co-worker offered to loan him the money to make a professional recording of some of them. When you begin to make your thoughts become real, you will find that events will happen and people will come into your life that will accelerate that process. That's part of the law of attraction too. Bob Newhart made the tape and sent it out to three hundred radio stations. Three of them responded, and pretty soon his stories were on the radio. He quit his accounting job and concentrated full time on inventing comic stories and recording them for the radio.

He wasn't an immediate success, however. One year he only made $1,100. He lived with his parents for years. Then finally a record company called him and offered him a contract to make a record. The only problem was, they wanted to record him live before an audience. He'd never been in a nightclub! Radio was the only medium he had used. But he scrambled and got himself a two-week gig at a motel lounge so that the company could make the recording. He won three Grammys the next year.

Some of you may be like that, possessed of such a potent passion that you already know what you should be doing. Some of you may be saying, "I don't have to go through this exercise. I can taste the hunger; I know what would make my life better. I just want to know how to get there. I can't seem to get started." I'm going to help you with that in the following chapters.

> *First find something you like to do so much you'd gladly do it for nothing; then learn to do it so well people are happy to pay you for it.*
>
> —Walt Disney

But I suspect that many of you are less certain. You may so often have simply forced yourself to ignore the things that make you passionate that you don't know what they are. You've taken on other people's passions—other people's goals, other people's burdens, other people's values—so completely that you don't know what you want. You're like the person who looks at the menu in the window but can't decide— never eaten that, don't like this, that one's fattening, that's too expensive, this is too rich—and walks away without sitting down to the table. Your diet might be the right one for you, but more likely you're starving yourself without even knowing what you're missing.

I know a guy who played basketball a lot when he was a teenager. But one day he came out with his ball at the usual time, took a few shots, and then just stopped and said, "I'm going home." When I asked him why he was leaving before he even was warmed up, he said, "I just realized that I was playing because I always do. But I don't really feel like it now." I asked him what he was going to do, and he said, "I don't know. I'll just have to figure it out." Sometimes you have to take a good look at yourself and ask, *Is this what I really want?* In fact, if you have to ask that question, you should probably be trying something else.

Priorities: What's Your First Choice?

Your **priorities** are more than just the things you need to do right away. Prioritizing means deciding *how* you live your life—it's like finding your style, your groove. You may want to be center stage as a performer, or you may prefer to work out of the limelight. You may be most excited when you're working with a group, or you may find that you accomplish things only by working alone. If you like to work with other people, you may need to be the leader or you may need to be the go-to person who gets the detail work done.

You might need complete freedom to create, or on the other hand, you might need a framework or a clear step-by-step plan. Some people like to work with their hands, and some people like to work with their heads. Think about whether you want to learn new things or just get on with doing something you already know about. Would money be a priority even when you had enough to live comfortably? Would you like to work for your community? Would you like to help people who are sick or deprived of something else?

Your most comfortable situation may be a combination of several of these. Probably, though, one style fits you best, and it is usually tied into your unique talents and abilities. As I said, I loved to perform for other people, and I quickly discovered that I loved speaking in public. Once I had graduated from seminary, I could have gone into a monastery and devoted myself to God that way. But actually, I wouldn't have been too happy. I can't imagine myself trying to do stand-up comedy with gestures so that I wouldn't break a vow of silence.

Your priorities will fine-tune the picture. How do you want to live? How do you want your body to look? Lots of friends or just a few? Several years ago, I found myself having to go through this work on myself. I was traveling all over the world speaking to groups, and let me tell you, it was exciting. But it was also a grind. I was traveling twenty-two, twenty-three, twenty-four days a month. One day I found myself looking up at the ceiling of another hotel room and thinking, *There's got to be more to life than this. I want to go to my kids' Little League games, I want to mix it up with my friends, I want to be home.* I had my priorities all wrong. And I had to stop and think how to balance my passions, my purpose, with my priorities. With a little work, I was able to reduce my traveling schedule and spend more time at home. And you know what? I actually enjoyed traveling more, because I was doing it the way I wanted to.

Your priorities change over time. You'll want to keep checking in with yourself, asking yourself if this is what you want and when you want it. You'll find too that when you start accomplishing your goals, that in itself will affect your priorities. Once you become a successful guitar player, you may not worry so much about looking good on the beach. Once you've renovated that room, you may find that do-it-yourself projects start to move up on your priorities list. In fact, everything in life will evolve. Even your purpose may change over time. Andrew Carnegie spent half his life making money and the other half giving it away. He was born poor, but once he was rich, he wanted to give back.

I'll tell you a little secret. You know the reason I was traveling so much? I was trying to be someone else. I had read that another motivational speaker was always on the road. I thought, *Well, I guess that's what*

I have to do. I'm not really doing my job unless I'm traveling all the time. There I was again, living my life by someone else's rules.

I learned my lesson, and I hope you learn my lesson too. Your goal may be the same as someone else's, but you have to accomplish it your way, with your abilities, your purpose, and your priorities. You were born an original, so why would you want to die a copy?

Make Your Ps a Priority

Let's look at those lists we drew up in the last chapter—the things you don't want and the things you do want. Divide them up into purpose, passions, and priorities. Maybe you'll think of more. As you become attuned to looking at your life in this way, you'll be able to pinpoint the things in your life that make it especially yours. That's what we're doing with the Ps—discovering what actions, feelings, and styles are unique and special to you. Once Selene is really feeding that purpose-driven hunger for a satisfying vocation, I suspect that her blahs will go away.

- Don't let other people decide how you are going to live your life.

- Think about what's important to you—how you want to make a difference in this world, what activities motivate you, and what situations make you the most comfortable and productive.

YOUR UTMOST LIVING JOURNAL

As before, only some of these questions will pertain to you, and there are hundreds of variations on these questions that will be specific to your needs and potentials. You may have very different responses in different parts of your life. Don't be afraid to admit to qualities that some others could find unfavorable—when you put them in the service of your utmost life, they will always, *always* be positive contributions.

Purpose

You may have explored this when thinking about the spiritual aspects of your life, because purpose is all about the things that make your spirit grow and give meaning to your world. Purpose may seem to evolve more than the other fundamental ingredients of an utmost life, but that is likely a matter of perspective rather than substance. As you accomplish goals, you may find that the goal itself simply was a means to a purpose. Purpose is about what you add to the world around you, what you give to other people, what stone you want to turn so that people will know that you passed this way.

If you had a million dollars to spend on something or someone other than yourself, what would you do?

_____

_____

_____

_____

Suppose you become accomplished in your dominant passion. How would you leave your mark with it? For instance, if you learned to play the piano, would you like to perform for others, write music, or record it for others' pleasure?

_____

_____

_____

If your friends or family were describing you to someone who didn't know you, what would you want them to say?

_____

_____

_____

Who has contributed the most to our world, and how have they done it?

_____

_____

_____

Passions

Your passions may be obvious to you, but you may have let them become buried in the busyness of life or other people's ideas. If they are not obvious, you will want to catch yourself in unguarded moments when you are not thinking about the duties and responsibilities that have become part of your life. Or you may simply have to create those moments, to force yourself to quiet all the other voices in your head and listen to your own. Remember that *anything* can be a passion that you can turn into your utmost life, from enjoying your pet to helping the sick.

What do you think about when you wake up in the morning?

_____

_____

_____

When you've finished your day's work, what do you turn to for pleasure and fulfillment?

_____

_____

_____

When you're talking with friends, what subject most excites and energizes you?

_____

_____

_____

_____

What would you do if you had all the time and money in the world and knew you couldn't fail at what you try?

_____

_____

_____

_____

Priorities

Your priorities are how you like to conduct your life. Let's look at some of those aspects of life we used in the previous worksheet.

Physical. Do you need a lot of sleep or just a little? Do you need to be very careful of what you eat (for reasons other than sheer weight gain)? Are you more energetic in the morning or the evening? Do you like warm weather, cool weather, or a mix? Is there a particular physical ability that you can make use of, or on the other hand, is there a physical limitation that you want to overcome?

_____

Personal. Do you absorb new things best by reading, listening, or seeing? Do you need to concentrate on one thing at a time or do you prefer variety and change? Do you like to do things fast and hard and then take a break, or do you prefer to go about your life steadily and consistently every day? Do you like calm or excitement?

Social. Do you like to be with people most of the time, with a few close friends, or mostly alone? Do you want to be in charge of what you do with other people, or would you prefer that everyone decide together? Do you try new things because of your friends or do you make new friends because you try new things? Would you rather do things for others or simply with others?

Professional. Are you a leader, a loner, or a team player? Do you like to start things and then move on to new projects, or do you like to see your efforts build and grow? Do you want to make a lot of money, do you want just enough to be comfortable, or is money not an issue at all?

Spiritual. Do you want to feel a spiritual dimension in everything you do, or is it something that supports you in the background of your life? Are you always seeking to understand more of the universe's purpose, or are you comfortable with the knowledge you have? Do you prefer to be with people who believe as you do, or are you stimulated by a variety of ideas?

3

Don't Let Your Can'ts
Cancel Your Wants

One day, as I'm heading into the diner for breakfast, I'm caught behind a family that seems to take up the entire entryway. The father is chubby and waddles from side to side with every step. What's really odd, though, is that his two sons and his wife also sway from side to side when they walk, even though they're not overweight. Puzzling over this, I'm finally waved over to a table. I walk past Jack, glad to see that he's sitting in a booth near a window, and greet him. "Nice to see you again, " he says. "I wish I could stop and talk some more, but I've got to go."

"Big date?"

"Actually, I have a job interview. I finally decided that I didn't have to answer phones all day if I really didn't want to."

As I'm sitting down, there is suddenly a hysterical yowl from the little girl in the large family. "No-o-o-o-o-o," she screams, "I don't want eggs! I want macaroni and cheese! *Macaroni and cheese!*" Her mother gradually calms her down, insisting all the while that she just can't have macaroni and cheese for breakfast.

Although I wouldn't want pasta for breakfast, I have to admire her honesty and forthrightness—and even that she won't take "can't" for an answer. Children can be infuriating, but sometimes it's just because they're not caught up in the habits and expectations that the rest of us are. Is a cheese omelet with home fries really all that much different from a plate of macaroni and cheese?

Don't Starve Your Dreams

We grow up and often we let all those can'ts lock the doors on us, keep us from what we want. We grow up and those can'ts get bigger until they are six foot ten and weigh three hundred pounds. Look at that one: *I can't leave my job unless I already have a job.* That's a big one. There's another one: *Can't get out of this bad relationship or else I'd be alone.* That one over there: *Can't have what I want because I'm not good enough*—that one is a giant can't. These can'ts are like big, mean-looking louts standing in front of the door to your utmost life. You can't step over that threshold because they make you nervous, afraid. *What if they try to stop me? What if they make me look foolish? What if they hurt me?*

All the while, our wants are being starved because of those giant can'ts. We don't start feeding the hunger that's inside us. *I want a better job, but I can't afford the training.* Starved out. *I want to be a success, but I can't afford to try and fail.* Starved out. Our wants become puny, undernourished things. Eventually they die. Unless you're dreaming those dreams, they will never be able to come true.

In order to live an utmost life you have let your wants grow until they overcome the can'ts. As we'll see in this chapter, sometimes a can't isn't at all what it seems to be. It may be a shouldn't or a daren't or even—be honest now—a don't want to.

"She'll learn," says the man at the table next me, nodding at the little girl. "Sometimes you just have to take what life dishes out. It's breakfast—you can't eat macaroni and cheese."

"Haven't you ever had a hunger for something so strong that you couldn't stop it?"

> *You will never be satisfied until you are working toward the purpose you were created to fulfill.*

"Not me," he says, setting his jaw. He's a big man, with graying hair and a nice suit. "I know what's good for me. Look, I sell life insurance. Do you think I grew up wanting to sell life insurance? Of course not. But it was my father's business and he had built up a fantastic trade. I would have been crazy to do what I wanted to do." He seems a little defensive about my question, which always makes me wonder if he hasn't thought about changing his life from time to time.

Carlos, as he introduces himself, has responded the way most of us would respond to the idea of looking at our lives in a new way. It's an overwhelming challenge, as every aspect of our lives would be transformed. For many people, it's too much even to think about now. "Maybe tomorrow," they say. And tomorrow turns into never. Change can be confusing and upsetting, even frightening. We say: "That's who I am. That's me, and who would I be if I weren't me?"

I know how it feels. When I was in the seventh and eighth grades I was the captain of the basketball team. So when I went to high school, I had my big Afro, my Converse high-tops, and my attitude. I just knew that I would be a star on the court. But in high school, there were all these kids from other schools. After the tryouts, the coach read off the names of the players who'd made it, and I waited for my name. He kept on reading off the names, but he didn't say mine. Then he finished reading the list and still he hadn't called my name. I hadn't made it. I walked home in a funk.

That was like having the rug pulled out from under me in terms of who I was. Change is hard. It really messed with my identity; I lost the thing that defined me. Change is hard, but I had to change. *Had* to change. I needed a new identity, the quicker the better. I spent a long time trying to figure out which group I fit into. I tried out all the talents I had—I used my energy, my humor, sports, dancing. It's not as if people didn't like me, but there were still times I felt like Sammy Davis Jr., who had to tap-dance his way into the Rat Pack. Sometimes I just didn't feel like being funny or dancing. I knew I hadn't found the place where I fit.

Drifting like that can make you miserable. In fear of drifting forever, people define themselves by a job, a family role, or another frame that only limits them. Once we do that, we put a big lock on the door to our dreams. "I'm a father," you say, "not a musician. I couldn't possibly start a new band now." Can't open that door—but really, you don't want to risk it.

We accept and even welcome what we've been handed, using up our time on earth when a great gift of following our purpose is out there waiting for us. Carlos has figured out where he fits—in the insurance business—and he's not about to give it up. But naturally, I'm curious.

"What was it that you wanted to do?" I ask.

"Ah, nothing. Never mind."

"No, really. I'd like to know."

"Well, I . . . No, it's ridiculous."

"Come on, I won't tell anybody."

"You better not. Not here. Because I wanted to be a chef."

"Really?"

"Sure. Why do you think I come here? The cook here, he uses real cream in the sauces. He uses sauces, for heaven's sake. Things like that. A little nutmeg in the savory omelets. This is a guy who knows how to cook, but he doesn't get crazy about it. Just the right thing in the right place."

If the creator had a purpose in equipping us with a neck, he surely meant us to stick it out.

—Arthur Koestler

I can see this man's purpose shining in his eyes right there. Not only that, but it's clear that he has touched and smelled and tasted his gift. It pains me to see someone who is ignoring their destiny, someone who is eating eggs when what they really want is macaroni and cheese, having a hamburger when what they really want is steak. How to unlock those locks? How to evict those louts from the door?

On the way to an utmost life, one of the things we all need to learn is to be fully alive every moment. I recently had the privilege of speaking at Café Oprah, where I had the equally rewarding privilege of having dinner with Björn Borg. We talked about life and tennis, especially those incredible matches with John McEnroe. I asked him, "Were there times when you felt like giving in?" He said, "That was never in my mind, or even in my vocabulary. I always played every single point as though it was the final point." I learned a lot from Björn Borg that night. I like that idea of playing every ball as if it's your last. That's how you should live your life—to the fullest, being fully present, fully feeling, and fully alive. That will take you to a very good place.

The Three Keys to Making Dreams Come True: Imagination, Focus, and Courage

Even if you have a clear purpose that you want to pursue, you still have to make it happen. Your dreams won't come true unless you make them. There are three basic building blocks in the nutritional pyramid for building strong dreams: imagination, focus, and courage. We spent a good part of the last chapter exercising the imagination, and I hope that's becoming more comfortable, more energizing for you. Imagination is the power that allows you to see your life as it will be. Imagination is what will unlock the locks. It can overcome all the can'ts there are in your mind. Imagination gives you the strength to overcome obstacles, to make excuses evaporate, and to envision the path to your future.

> *Imagination is everything—it is the*
> *preview of life's coming attractions.*
>
> —Albert Einstein

As we talk, I learn that Carlos has exercised his imagination so much that I can feel its power. He has spent years cooking at home for his family and friends, and even taken some courses. When he describes how different ingredients combine, the details are so vivid that even I can taste the result. He talks about the kind of menu he would have if— just if, of course—he had his own restaurant. He can tell me how many people he would need in the kitchen and why his cooking would be different from any other chef's in town. He's constantly being asked, and thanked, for his opinion on an Internet chat group about food and cooking. Even his wife says he should be a professional. "But that's just her talking, you know, God love her."

Carlos has instinctively feasted on the single most important ingredient for making his dream happen—imagining the goal in vivid and in-depth detail. When you've fixed your sights on something, read everything you can find about it. Talk to people who are doing what you want to be doing. Make a dream board of pictures and articles about what you're aiming at. Carlos has made his dream board in his head.

"Did you try cooking for a living?" I ask Carlos.

"I could never do that. I've got a family to feed. I can't just give up my job and start cooking in some joint at minimum wage." There's that giant can't—*I can't transform my life.*

"Who's asking you to give up your job?"

"Besides, what good would it do me? I sell life insurance. That's what I do." There's another one.

"Carlos, there was a guy in Seattle, Washington, who worked for Boeing for twenty years. As soon as he could retire, he went to cooking school in New York and started his own business making cured ham and salami."

"Yeah, that Batali guy. I read about him. His son's a famous chef."

"But he had been learning about food for years before that. He prepared, he studied, he made himself ready to take advantage of his opportunity. Imagine how good it felt to finally use all that preparation."

"Yeah. Yeah, I'm sure that would be excellent."

Carlos the insurance salesman also has the second essential for building strong dreams: focus. Carlos has the ability to concentrate on a goal and pull together the necessary ingredients. Despite working eight hours a day at a job that he doesn't really like, he has devoted every spare moment to his passion. He hasn't let himself sit in front of the television complaining that he never has time to do the things he wants to do. Over time, his focus on his hobby took on its own momentum—the more he learned, the more he wanted to try out. The more he cooked, the more he wanted to learn about cooking. The more he learned, the more he started inventing his own dishes, unleashing his own creativity. Focus like that is what turns your dream into a reality.

> *Luck is a matter of preparation meeting opportunity.*
>
> —Oprah Winfrey

So why hasn't Carlos become a chef? Because he hasn't yet found the third essential: courage. Now, I'm not talking about the kind of courage you need to wrestle alligators or topple evil dictators or lead troops into battle. Those are admirable things to do, but most of us need that kind of courage only rarely, if ever.

The kind of courage I'm talking about is part and parcel of everyday life, and everyone has it in some measure. It's the courage to do what you have to do even when you know it will be difficult. It's the courage to try something new, the courage to get out of your old ruts and old ways of thinking. It's the courage, most of the time, to simply be able to say, "I'm afraid of looking for a new job—what if I'm rejected?" or "I'm afraid of giving up smoking—what if I fail?" Once they acknowledge that it's fear—not anything they can see or touch or that could fight back, but just fear—that is preventing them from changing, most people are already on the road to a better life. It's like the drunk who stands up and says, "I am an alcoholic." That's the first step.

That's what has kept Carlos from realizing his dream. He has to confront those two giants: *Can't change my life* and *That's not who I am.*

I'd like to see if I can help him. "You're not really just an insurance salesman," I say. "You're an insurance salesman who's a terrific cook. Are you a terrific cook?"

"Well, I . . . well, there are some people who have said this."

"You say it."

"Come on."

"No, I just want to hear you say it." He looks at me like I'm crazy. "OK, so I'm crazy. Humor me."

"I'm a . . . a cook." I look at him. "A terrific cook."

You'll be surprised at what saying something out loud can do.

He smiles. "I am a terrific cook." That giant *That's not what I am* is starting to look very nervous. As Carlos clarifies his thoughts and focuses on the positive, his vision becomes stronger.

All things come to him who hustles
while he waits.

—Thomas Edison

Next step: do one small thing. "So what about doing some cooking on the side?"

"I can't just do anything I feel like doing anytime I feel like it. I got a wife to take care of."

"But she's already said you should be a professional."

"Yeah, but it would be irresponsible."

Carlos has probably been told all his life that the man has to be the breadwinner, that a man's got to do what a man's got to do, that he should think of others before himself, and on and on. In other words, he's been told everything but the one thing that would help make his life fulfilling—about listening to that inner voice that speaks your passion and purpose. But there's no reason he couldn't start to blaze a new trail in his life. I can't resist urging him a little further.

"Did you ever have a dinner for some of your best customers?"

"Oh, yeah, I take 'em over to the Italian place on . . ."

"No, I mean did you ever cook for them?"

"Cook for them? What . . . what if they hated it?"

There's that other giant, *What if I fail?* We're going to talk much more about failure, not just imagined failure, but the real thing, and you'll see that it's not the bogeyman that it seems. But before you're ready to cope with real failure, you need the courage to let go of that imagined failure that hasn't even happened yet.

Courage is the third essential for building your dream and making it come true. Courage in everyday life is not about facing danger or risking your life. But it is about taking initiative, recognizing when something that seems like an obstacle really turns out to be fear of failure—fear of the challenge, fear of ridicule, even fear of success.

> *Life shrinks or expands according to one's courage.*
>
> —Anaïs Nin

The other big fear is fear of change, of becoming something different, unknown. It may come from ignorance—some people just haven't realized that the Anything Is Possible Network is on the air full time. They don't know what the opportunities are, and even when they do, they say, "*People like me don't do that.*" Others simply refuse to do what comes naturally because their father or their mother or their sister or their brother already did it. Fear, pride, and ignorance can all eat away at your courage, but if you listen to your God idea, you have a force in your heart that will feed your courage and give you the strength to face down your fears. God does not teach you to swim in order to let you drown. He does not want you to be a could-have-been. He will find ways to open your eyes to see beyond the barriers you have erected.

Like many of us, Carlos thinks he is not good enough, smart enough, dedicated enough, or something else enough. For some people this goes way beyond the fear of failure—they are *sure* they're going to fail. Even if they succeed at something once, they know they'll fail the next time, or the time after that. What you need to know is that failure is the first step on the road to success.

> *This thing that we call failure is not the falling down, but the staying down.*
>
> —Mary Pickford

You don't remember when you were a year old and learning how to walk, but you've seen it often enough with the children in your life. They get up, they fall down, they get up, they fall down, they get up, they walk, they fall down, they get up, they walk. They can't say it, but they know their destiny is to walk, and they *will* walk. It's as natural to them as breathing. That's how it is with your destiny. Failure, as Henry Ford said, is just a way of finding out how to do it better. Carlos needs to stop anticipating failure and to start focusing on what is real and powerful in him—his purpose, his God idea.

I tell Carlos that his clients won't hate his dinner if he lets his purpose guide him, because I know that his purpose will not fail him—it won't let him fail. He only needs to use his imagination so that he can look beyond the limits he has put on himself and see the unlimited potential he has.

"Tim," says Carlos, "you talk a pretty good line. Maybe you should be the one selling insurance. Meanwhile, I'll be planning what's for dinner."

I can tell that he's beginning to let himself draw courage from his purpose. It's a great feeling, one that you'll want to feel again and again. At first, you may not see this spirit in yourself very often; even once a week might be rare. But as you begin to make more conscious, deliberate choices about what you're doing every day, you'll probably find yourself feeling alive in new ways. No one else can do it for you, and excuses will only take you further from it. But nourish that purpose-driven hunger, and you'll be stronger every day.

There's another kind of courage that is crucial to your success, and that is the courage to keep trying. Whether you call it persistence or perseverance, it's really faith in your purpose and the resolve to just throw all your excuses in the garbage. One of my favorite excuses is that there's a better time coming soon. Even when we know what we want to be doing—what we should be doing in order to fulfill our purpose on this earth—it's easy to put off doing that work until tomorrow. Or next Wednesday. In just a few weeks, things will be better.

You're going to start a diet, and you're going to start it on Monday because Monday is the beginning of the week, and usually you've eaten too much on the weekend anyway, so by Monday you'll have stuffed yourself so much that you've added two pounds to however much weight you have to lose today.

Or next week you'll get paid, so you'll have some money to buy whatever it is that seems crucial to your self-improvement. Or two weeks from now, your mother-in-law will have finally gone home and you won't have that aggravation anymore. Next month, you'll be stronger, smarter, tougher, and more determined. Whew! Won't that be a time!

Well, I think you're already strong, smart, tough, and determined. I think you might as well start today because tomorrow you'll still be that strong, smart, determined person and the sooner you start to use the gifts that God gave you, the better you'll feel. And come Monday, if you haven't started to use those powers, you may think that the best time has passed, and now there's no point in even trying. At least until the Monday after that.

To persevere, trusting in what hopes he has, is courage in a man.

—Euripides

Can'ts in Your Pants?

There are many, many reasons why we feel we can't do something, but there are seven that stand out. We've looked at two that come from inside—fear of changing who we are and fear of failure. What's the next big one? Come on, you know this. Money. Right now you're probably thinking you can't afford to do the thing that will make you truly deeply satisfied. Not only that, you can't afford to be able to afford it—you can't take time away from this, you can't save on that. Think about what you're saying—you can't afford to be *able* to afford the thing you most crave and need?

I don't believe it. I think you can't afford *not* to. You can't afford to spend your life going from sleep to work to home to sleep to work to home over and over again. Isn't there something in your life that you don't need to afford? Seriously, did you have to afford that new suit you saw last week? Did you have to afford that new cell phone that everybody thinks is so cool? Your balance sheet needs to take into account a longer term than just the end of the month. If you want to live an utmost life, you can't afford *not* to learn new things. You can't afford *not* to do new things, to be new things. You'll never make a better investment.

My first experience at finding money to satisfy a hunger came after chasing an ice cream vendor on a hot summer day. As soon as my friends heard the music of the truck, they shouted, "Ice cream, let's go!" I pedaled my bike as fast as the rest of them, even though I wasn't sure where we were going or what all the excitement was about.

When I saw those rainbow-colored Popsicles, chocolate fudge bars, and ice cream sandwiches painted on the side of the truck, my eyes grew as big as silver dollars. But then I realized I was going to need a dollar to buy one of the frozen treats my friends were already slurping. I didn't have a dollar. I watched as each of my friends reached in his pocket for the coins he needed to pay the ice cream man. Suddenly, all eyes were on me. "What are you going to have, Tim?"

I fumbled for an excuse. "I . . . I'm going to eat soon, so I'm not going to get anything right now." Everyone believed me—or, come to think of it, I suppose no one really cared why I wasn't having any—but that day changed my life. Acting casual, I asked a few questions and I learned that my friends all had money in their pockets because of something I had never heard of—an allowance. One of my friends said, "Yeah, I have to do things around the house every day, but then my parents give me spending money for the week."

All this time I'd been ignorant, but now I knew that I was on to something that could be a very good deal for me. Since then, I have learned that money is never the problem—the only problem comes when you don't think there is a way to get it. Believe that you can do it. Use your imagination, focus, and courage, and you will get it. Soon you will know it will come—call it faith if you want.

There are ways to earn money, ways to save money, and ways to get money. I can't tell you how many millionaires borrowed money to start the thing that made them rich, famous, or just fulfilled. Money can be a real obstacle, not just an excuse, but it is an obstacle that can always be overcome. I know that some of you don't have the money now, but what can you do until then? In the next chapter, when we discuss setting goals that will take you on the road to your dream, we'll see how to overcome obstacles like this one.

Live within your means, but dream beyond your means—and then live up to your dreams.

The fourth can't is our responsibilities to family and loved ones. Carlos felt it so strongly that he had never even discussed expanding his cooking hobby with his wife. Is it possible that she would deny a reasonable request from her husband? I doubt it. They can plan together how to make Carlos's God idea come true. Too often, we are afraid of being too self-important, of singling ourselves out and taking the responsibility for changing our partners' lives—and our lives. In other situations, people may be afraid that rejection would force them to make a decision about a friendship, a marriage, or a partnership. It takes courage to face that, but later I'll talk about building a support network around you that will cushion you against this kind of shock.

"Tim," you're asking, "when are we going to get down to work? You keep saying that we'll learn something in the next chapter, or a later chapter." Yes, you're right. Some people can see their dream, feel their purpose, and be hungry enough to start work right away. Those people may not need to spend as much time as another person on the reasons they haven't started living an utmost life.

If you know already what's holding you back, if none of these fears are holding you back and you're impatient to get on with it, then you can go to the next chapter. But make a note about impatience in your book—in order to transform your life, you will need to work hard, and if you skip a step, it can come back to haunt you. You may find that there is more than one thing holding you back, and find yourself back here, but that will be progress too.

> *The man who complains about the way the ball bounces is likely the one who dropped it.*
>
> —Lou Holtz

The fifth can't is feeling that we have to do it all on our own. You want to accomplish your goal on your own, without anyone else's help. The result is that you don't do anything until you've learned absolutely everything you need to know, earned the money that you need rather than borrowed it, or learned how to be two people so that you can do all the jobs, preferably at once. You want to plan the menu, buy the food, cook the dishes, serve the patrons, manage the accounts, and renovate the dining room. All by yourself.

On the other side of the same coin, maybe you can't progress because you need to find the one person, or two people, who would have exactly what you need in order to get started. A teacher, a supporter, an angel, a mentor, a good audience. They will have the finances, the expertise, the energy, or the steadfastness to keep you working.

Actually, both of these excuses, turned into strategies and used properly, are part of living an utmost life. We do need to learn, and we do need to find help and accept it. As I said, we will talk about building that support network, which provides both internal and external support—both the emotional help you need and the finances, knowledge, and connections. However, these things become excuses when you insist on all or nothing. If you decide that nothing will happen until you have gained everything you need or that nothing will happen until you have the right people to help you—well, then, nothing will happen.

Take the Can'ts off the Menu

What is keeping you from living your dream? Write down everything you can think of. When you think of an obstacle, imagine for a moment that it's overcome. If it's money, imagine what you would do if someone gave you the money. If it's time, imagine that someone will help you out to give you enough free time to work on your dream. Then ask yourself what other obstacle could keep you from being a star. Imagine that obstacle overcome. When you come to the last obstacle, imagine yourself pursuing your passion, fulfilling your goal. Make that vision become real until you can feel it in your bones and muscles, your heart and your soul.

Then get way down deep or way outside yourself and tell yourself how you can overcome the obstacles, the emotions, the worries, the lacks. You may not be able to overcome them all today, or tomorrow, or next week, or next year. But let me assure you that you will overcome them. You will make history in overcoming them. You will make your history.

- Vividly envisioning your goal is the key to realizing it.
- Don't let anything distract you from your goals.
- Have the courage to trust in your dreams.

YOUR UTMOST LIVING JOURNAL

Think about the dreams you've dreamed during your life. Right now, you may have trained yourself to ignore those dreams and focus on practical, everyday kinds of accomplishments. One of the things I'd like you to do is to unlearn that narrow focus. When you were a kid you had dreams that you had to give up for good reasons. I wanted to be a basketball player, but I learned that I wasn't as good as I thought I was. Now I've realized a completely different kind of dream—but it was just as unlikely as me being a basketball player. Try to remember what it felt like to believe that you could be anything you wanted to be, and apply it to the activities you love to do most right now. Dream of success, acclaim, and honors. Write down what you're thinking—not because you're going to make it happen, though you may, but because dreaming big is a skill you need to exercise.

Now you'll start to nail down the menu that will take you to your first utmost meal. I will use one example, losing weight, as a model. Although that might seem an obvious one, I think it will help show how all the aspects of your life play into one another.

1. Pick out one or more of the passions in your list from the previous worksheet, one of the things you want to turn into a goal, either short-term or long-term.

Passion: Losing weight

2. How do your priorities enable you to fulfill this passion?

Physical: Getting more exercise

Personal: I like to make a big change all at once and stick to it

Social: I like to do things with other people

Professional: Can't think of anything

Spiritual: I will have more time to give to my friends and family

3. Is this passion a part of your purpose in life?

Purpose: I want to contribute to my children's life—losing weight will help me live longer and provide a good example for them

Now try it yourself with one of your passions.

Perhaps the most important skill you'll learn on the road to your utmost life is visualization. Like any other skill, you'll become better at it the more you use it, but it can be difficult at the beginning. I'll give you a series of exercises that can help you train yourself for the more difficult tasks later.

1. The easiest way to begin is to start with something that you're familiar with. For instance, imagine what you will be doing later today, or this evening. I'm not suggesting that you try to invent anything—just think of what you usually do, step by step. You might think, *Well, I'll go home, have dinner, watch some television, read a little, and then go to bed.* Wait a minute—you didn't visualize *everything.* Go back—would you change your clothes, look through the mail, look in the refrigerator? What clothes would you put on? What television shows are you going to watch? What are you going

to read? See how detailed you can make your visualization. (Warning: this can be a sobering exercise—but don't be hard on yourself, just accept your life as it is.)

2. When you feel comfortable about visualizing your usual routine, visualize some activity that you enjoy but don't do every day. If you like sewing, for instance, think about what you would like to sew. Try to feel how it feels when you're doing it. Think about the satisfaction you feel when that piece of work is finished. Even if you're just imagining watching television, you can visualize what you might be watching, how often your mind wanders, whether you grab a snack at the commercial, and so forth.

3. Now that you've practiced things you know, it's time to move on to something you don't know. Imagine one of your favorite activities, but on an occasion when it's as wonderful and satisfying as it could possibly be. If you jog, for instance, imagine how it would be if your legs weren't stiff and if your lungs felt as though they could expand forever. Imagine the swing of your legs, the smoothness of your stride, the pleasure you feel at doing something as well as you can.

Focus, like imagination, can be trained. Think of those times when you were so involved with something that time flew by. What were those activities? What made them so engrossing? Keep a log of them.

Focus can also be a refreshing exercise in itself. Meditation is a well-known exercise in religion, but it's not just for devotional purposes. Meditation is really nothing more than focused thinking. Take five minutes to focus on something simple—your breathing, or a favorite image, or the memory of a favorite person. Set a timer so that you don't have to think about whether you've spent five minutes, and try just to think about the thing you've decided to focus on. If your mind starts to wander, don't feel bad—just bring it back to the subject. As you feel more comfortable and in control of your thoughts, focus on something in your life that you would like to change.

You may feel that courage is something you have to get from the Wizard of Oz, as the Cowardly Lion did. But remember what the Wizard said to the lion—all he needed was a testimonial. Of course it's an amusing scene, but maybe it's closer to the truth than it initially seems. I'm sure there have been times in your life when you did something that took courage—you took a physical risk, perhaps, or stood up to someone in authority. Think about those incidents, even if they happened long ago. What was it that allowed you to face down your fears? Was it your own belief in yourself? Your excitement about accomplishing something? The encouragement of friends? The point is that you've done it before and you can do it again—all you need is the right situation.

Finally, think about the things in your life that are preventing you from doing things you want to do—those can'ts in your life. Just list them for now.

OBJECTIVE	CAN'T	SOLUTION

4

. . .

Listen to Yourself

We've talked about the basics that go into creating an utmost life: purpose, passions, and priorities—the 3 Ps, which define your goals and how you want to get to them. We've also talked about the attitudes that will keep you on the path—imagination, focus, and courage. Now it's time to take the first steps toward transforming your life, and for that you'll need some specific tools, which is what we'll discuss in this chapter. If I told you how to bake an apple pie, even if I gave you all the ingredients, you wouldn't have much success unless I also gave you the tools—rolling pin, pie pan, pie weights, and an oven.

The first step in finding your God idea is to start looking for it. Even if you began this book sincerely wanting to change your life, sincerely searching for the wonder that's in you, you may have been just turning pages so far, flipping through the menu, waiting for something or someone to make the choice for you. It's like when you go out for dinner and everybody always asks everybody else what they're having before they decide. You might be thinking, *Maybe Tim will suggest what I should do next, so that I don't have to do all that writing and thinking and stuff.* You may not even be aware that you're doing that. But unless you've started to feel that urgency, that sense that there's a new life waiting for you around the corner, then that's what's going on. When you do feel that urgency, it's so exciting and energizing that I couldn't stop you even if I wanted to.

> *You learn in life that the only person you can really correct and change is yourself.*
>
> —Katharine Hepburn

Of course there's no way I can tell you what you should be doing and you probably know that. They have to be your answers, your purpose, your passions. No one else can serve them up for you.

Divine Desperation

I was lucky enough to find my purpose early, and to find it right at home. My family was not only close-knit and God-fearing, they were also hard drinkers and sometime fighters. They'd get together on the weekend and it was like a contest to see who could drink the most and who could cause themselves the most embarrassment. One Saturday night, they were at it again, carrying on and talking about things that don't matter. I started saying to my sister that I didn't want to grow up that way. I wanted to make a difference in the world. I wanted to make it a better place not just for myself, but for my family and everyone else around me. I wanted to be a history maker and a world shaker. I wanted to make an impact on the neighborhood I grew up in. I wanted to help kids who needed a hand up and out of that "almost" place. I realized that I didn't have to be the way my family had always been.

My sister said she thought that was a great idea, but she was smart enough not to stop there. She reminded me about the friend of hers who won a silver medal at the Olympics in swimming. She didn't do it by dreaming about it. She would hit the alarm clock at five in the morning and go to the pool to practice. Then after school she was back in the pool again for another couple of hours. I used to wonder if her hair ever had a chance to dry.

> *To business that we love, we rise be-times, and go to it with delight.*
>
> —William Shakespeare

The point my sister was making was that if I was going to accomplish anything, I had better get desperate about it. I would have to do a lot of things that were new to me and even new to my family. I would have to graduate and go to seminary, and there'd be difficult days ahead. In fact, they were much harder than I had imagined they'd be. But I had taken that first step. I had made the decision that I was going to live my life by design rather than default; I had decided to take control of my destiny. I was desperate to take control of my destiny. That good desperation provided the key to change: motivation.

Was I special? I would say that I was special only in the way that all of us are special—fearfully and wonderfully made, as the Bible says. I was not especially favored. Remember, I was not the smartest kid in the class—I went to remedial reading classes in junior high school. I was a good athlete, as I said, until those other guys left me in the dust. I wasn't getting anywhere doing comedy routines for my friends.

Perhaps I was special in that I lost my father just when he might have helped me along the path to adulthood. Rather than being able to follow his—or anyone else's—guidance, I had to do it on my own. I spent years trying to figure out who I was. Even later, in seminary, I was not one of the crowd. I was special only in what I didn't have. But I was given much.

> *As long as I have a want, I have a reason for living.*
>
> —George Bernard Shaw

I was given divine desperation, which is not panic, not weakness, not frenzy, and not worry. It's a determination to do what needs to be done in order to be the person you want to be. I was young enough that I didn't stop to think that it might be hard, that there would be so much to learn and so many things to do. We could all use more of that child-like faith and fearlessness. The most important thing I can tell you is that you have all the talents and tools you need to become a world shaker and a history maker. All you have to do is to realize that you have them and have the confidence and the desire to put them to work.

Stop, Look, and Listen

If you haven't found your purpose in life yet, don't worry. Life can be busy, noisy, and confusing. There's always too much to do and not enough time to do it in, right?

Half right. Yes, life *can* be that way. But now you're going to take control of your life, and the first thing you're going to say is that your life is not going to be that way. It will be busy when you want it to be. It will be noisy when you're making the noise. But it won't be confusing because you know where you're going and how to get there. You're going to start your utmost life by checking out of the noise and bustle and busyness and finding some quiet.

> *To know your ruling passion, examine your castles in the air.*
>
> —Richard Whately

You have to stop, if only for a while, all the usual chores and duties and appointments in your life. We can get so busy that we become human doings, not human beings. And the more we do, the more people tell us what we should be doing. Friends, family, co-workers—everybody has an opinion about what we should do with our lives. Sometimes other people have told you the same thing so often that you think it's your own idea. That's part of the problem. As often as not, their opinions are about their lives, not yours. Of course it's important to listen to people, but you have to sift through what they're saying and take away the things that can help *you.*

Sometimes we're forced to take that break for ourselves, and it can be a lucky thing. Ron Meyer, now head of Universal Studios, was a poor kid who grew up in West Los Angeles, the son of German immigrants. He dropped out of high school, couldn't find a job, and spent a lot of his time shooting pool. Finally, he signed up with the Marines because he was attracted by their boxing program.

Then he got the best break of his life. He came down with the measles and was quarantined for two weeks. He had nothing to do, so his mother sent him a couple of books to read. One was about a Hollywood talent agent. After that, he says, "I realized that I was no longer that idiot kid I had been, and I wanted to change my life."

He had no degree, no experience in the movie business, and no training. He went around to all of the talent agencies in town and asked for any kind of a job at all. "Everyone said no to me. I didn't have a formal education. I came from no influence, no money. There was no obvious reason to give me a job." But he wouldn't give up, now that he had a goal. Besides, he says, "I couldn't afford to fail. I needed to make money." He worked as a busboy and short-order cook. He cleaned grease off duplicating machines. He sold shoes. "Once I got a job, I put all I had into it," says Meyer. "When I was a busboy, I wanted to be the best busboy."

He was working in a clothing store when the Paul Kohner Agency called him, remembering him as the kid who would take any job at any salary. He became a messenger there, at $75 a week. He became an agent. He started his own agency. Once he saw that success was possible, he was driven to achieve it. Ron Meyer has achieved things beyond his wildest childhood dreams, and all because he had to take a time-out. What makes him special is that he made the most of that time-out. He had the courage to make a choice and the persistence to stick with it.

It's time to get away from it all, time to take a day to break away from all the habits and thoughts that have been keeping you down. It's not only that you deserve a break today, you need to affirm that you are making a break—making a break for yourself. By taking a step out of your everyday routines, your everyday life, your everyday ideas, you will be taking the first step toward a richly rewarding, exciting, and fulfilling life. You're telling the world and most especially telling yourself that things are going to be different from now on.

It's time to take a look at your life, survey the landscape, read through the whole menu. Then you're going to listen so that you can hear the voice that's in your head and your heart. Let me warn you, though, nobody is going to start talking in your head in the tones of James Earl Jones. When that voice speaks to you, it's going to speak in your voice.

So one fine day when you have no pressing appointments or tasks, take a personal day. Call in sick if you have to, since this is a day to improve your mental health. Besides, it's not a day off; you'll be working. And I would bet you'll go back to work with a new energy.

Don't plan your day ahead of time: rather, plan to be unplanned. You might want to leave the house so that you're not distracted by chores, the computer, the television, or any of the other busyness that fills our lives. Let your mind be free, and let me suggest some fields where it can wander. This won't necessarily be easy for some of you—even Oscar Wilde said, "To do nothing at all is the most difficult thing in the world." But sometimes you have to clear out a space before you can find the place you need to be. I don't mean to suggest you're going to decide on your life's work in a day, but you can attune your mind to searching out the thing, or things, that give you a feeling of fulfillment and joy.

You can make your break in the company of someone else, and I know that many people have an easier time talking out their ideas rather than writing them down. But that person must know in advance what the day is all about—you. And you don't want to be distracted from you. If you don't know anyone who can take the time, imagine that you are having a conversation with someone who is deeply concerned about your future success. Keep your notebook handy with your lists of wants and don't wants, now sorted into the 3 Ps: purpose, passions, and priorities. You've also made some notes about the obstacles in your way. See how much progress you've made already?

First, you're going to look at your life, take inventory of what's in the pantry. Spend some time thinking about the various aspects of your life—your body, your character, your home life, your work life, the things that allow you to escape from work. Think about how you spend your time; you might be surprised at how much time you spend on things you don't care about. Think about how you spend your money; you might make the same kind of discovery. You should be or become comfortable with how you look—you don't have to be Brad Pitt or Angelina Jolie, but you can still be comfortable with what people see when they look at you. Think about your friendships and other personal relationships. Think about what you like to do and what you're good at doing.

While there may be parts of your life you want to work on more than others, none of them should blind you to the others. Now is the time to be as honest with yourself as possible. It's not easy, for several reasons. For one, when we think about ourselves, too often we wind up beating ourselves up for faults and failings. We get stuck in things that we find shameful, upsetting, or unattractive about ourselves.

We would rather speak ill of ourselves than not talk about ourselves at all.

—La Rochefoucauld

Being honest means seeing the good as well as the bad. In fact, another reason it's hard to be honest is that we beat ourselves up about characteristics that are not really bad in themselves. They are simply how we are at a given time and a given place—not all the time, not every time. You may be lazy about doing the housework but bursting with energy for gardening. You may not be able to spend time planning your week, but you can make four of your friends rearrange their schedules so that you can all get together.

Dwelling on your negatives is not really being honest with yourself. Are you letting your negatives define you? Are you writing a label for yourself? Are you letting your past determine your future? Don't bother with that.

One of the most interesting people I ever got a chance to talk to is Robert Downey Jr. We've had many great talks in restaurants and diners, and one fantastic talk in particular about not giving up. Robert is a great example of someone who has decided to live beyond the tags, the labels, that people have put on him. Labels have their own power—they tell you the content of what's inside, or how to use it, or its value. If you're holding a can that's labeled "Sprite," you're sure about what's inside. You know it's not Coke or water. We do the same thing with people. When somebody is labeled "drug addict" or "loser," we just assume we know what's inside them.

And if I've been given a label, I might start to think that way about myself. Just the way I was "class clown" until Mr. Probert made me respect myself. What I love about Robert is that he never gave in to the labels completely, even when he was on the cover of *Newsweek* for the challenges he has so openly talked about. I'm sure there were times he felt so weak that he couldn't fight it, or even days when he would give in, but in the end he knew he was greater than the labels put on him.

There was a greatness in him that needed to come out. I think of that as the real you making a demand on the you that you've become. I'm proud of Robert, proud of the fact that he decided not to sit or settle in his setback. I spent several days with him, Tobey Maguire, and Michael Douglas on the set of *The Wonder Boys* and it was clear Robert had let life and God bring him his comeback.

So if you've labeled yourself, or if other people have, tear those tags off. Remember, you are taking a break today. You are making a break for life today. This day is not about confession, it's about progression. When we were talking, Selene said to me, "I don't admit this to just everyone, but I'm lazy." But when Selene talked about the challenges and difficulties of putting all the pieces of that film poster together into an eye-catching design, she had more energy than two Selenes. She spent hours on that project and didn't even feel spent when it was finished; she felt energized. So—and I think this is true for many people— there are two Selenes. One of them had deep wells of get-up-and-go because she was doing something that fulfilled her. The other tired easily and didn't feel like making the effort for anything. But that was the Selene who felt no excitement about her work.

> *No one can make you feel inferior*
> *without your consent.*
>
> —Eleanor Roosevelt

If she really were lazy and that was interfering with her purpose in life, she could make that a priority for change. If drink or drugs are taking control of your life, you'll want to put that at the top of the list of things you want to change, because you want to be in control. And if you want to be, you can. Even the twelve-step programs agree that quitting anything—smoking, drugs, drinking—is ultimately something you have to want to do yourself. But the thing I want you to remember is that just because you have made mistakes, you are not a mistake. Just because you've developed bad habits doesn't mean that you're in the habit of being bad. In other chapters, we'll work hard on developing techniques and strategies for dealing with negative thoughts. But this day starts by making a break. You will change whatever is holding you back into what will bring you back. You will be renewed, redeemed, and refreshed.

Discovering Your Dream

Once you've thought about your talents and abilities, it's time to start figuring out where to apply them. There are several techniques and tools you can use to find out where your dream lives. One is writing down the times you've succeeded, the times you've felt happy, the people who have complimented you and what they praised. These experiences hold the deep truth of your life. Go back all the way, to your childhood. Remember how it was when you were a child and you woke in the morning? There was so much to do, so much ground to cover. You jumped out of bed and dove into your toys, got some breakfast, watched some cartoons, and you were off. When a friend shared a new toy or gadget with you, you didn't hesitate. If there was a new place to see, you went there. You had so much life and energy. Your life was built on enthusiasm.

When we grow up we substitute duty for enthusiasm. We take on responsibilities and chores that we don't really care about. The ground of our life gets smaller and smaller until we have barely enough to get by on. We forget what it was like when excitement was the color of the day, the taste of the meal, the motor of life. But there are still moments when we are taken out of ourselves by excitement, transported by enthusiasm. Thinking about those moments is a good way to start this day.

Another technique is to imagine going back to your twentieth (or thirtieth or fortieth—it's never too late) reunion. Imagine going there because you are proud of what you've accomplished and you want everyone to know about it. You want the superior kids to know that they were wrong about you. If you were Charlie Brown, you'd want the pretty red-haired girl to admire your achievements and finally, *finally* notice you. Don't worry about sounding boastful or describing things that are small—no achievement is too inconsequential if it's important to you.

> *If you want to be respected by others,*
> *the great thing is to respect yourself.*
>
> —Fyodor Dostoevsky

Or you might look in the opposite direction. When have you felt energized? When have you felt lifted out of yourself? When have you thought, "Wow, that time went by fast"? See if you can remember.

Here's another technique: think of the different purposes that people could have for their lives—money, fame, artistic success, being a good parent. You may have already written down purposes that you want to pursue, but try out some others in addition. Make them become real in your mind. Imagine how it would be if those things, things you love, were the reason for your existence. Think about how your life might change if you were living according to that purpose. Imagine that someone is writing a history of the world and they are writing about what you added to it.

Imagine the mayor of your town giving you an award for that purpose. Imagine your children saying, "My father made me capable and he made me care," or "My mother gave me love and made me able to love." If you find that you just can't commit to the purpose you chose for the day, you'll have learned something. In the days to come, pick one at the beginning of each new morning and think about it during the day. Give it a test drive. You may want to modify it or just move on to the next one. But keep on trying them.

Think about the moments in your life that have stuck with you. Think about the people in your life who have affected you, either for better or for worse. Think about what your parents made you care about, for better or for worse. Now that you have the urge for a change, ask yourself what these people would say to you, what those people would urge you to do.

All of these techniques are ways of finding out where you want to go with your life, and of separating the beliefs and activities that really stir your soul from the ones that other people—or movies or books or authority figures—are trying to sell to you. There's one that's right for you, for your life at this moment, and when you discover it and commit to it, motivation, courage, and focus will follow.

Love and Money—but What's the Real Reward?

Some of you may find yourselves saying, "If I could just find one person for me, one life partner, then I would be able to do anything." Well, think about that for a moment on your day off. I'm the last person to minimize the importance of love—God's love is what makes our lives possible, and the people in my life who've loved me are worth their weight in gold. But when you say that one person's love will make your life worth living, what you're really saying is that you're expecting *someone else* to make it possible for you to do things. Now, while I agree that a loved one's support and care can be a tremendous help, the only person who can change your life is you.

If you're looking for a life partner who will sacrifice him- or herself for you, then you're not there yet. You're just a half-person. And if you go out looking while you're a half-person, you'll attract another half-person. It's like saying to someone, "Oh, you're not dating the real me. I'm really a terrific person. When I'm not depressed, I'm a barrel of laughs." You need to learn to be a stronger, better person with more character so that you can start attracting stronger, better people. Once you are a whole person, you'll start attracting other whole people who will enrich your life instead of just filling a hole in it.

On the other hand, you may mean that you want to find someone to whom you can devote your life—perhaps your calling really is to be the someone who's there for someone else, not as a sacrifice but as a fulfillment of your life's purpose. Follow that thought through. Imagine what it would be like to give your life to someone else, to let someone else be your support and your compass. Imagine what that life would be. Would you find complete fulfillment in denying your other priorities and passions? What things about you would that other person have to accept? You may find that there are things you simply couldn't give up—and you will learn a great deal from that.

If I am not for myself, who will be for me? If I am only for myself, what am I?

—Hillel

Like love, money can seem an end in itself, and it is certainly something you will want to think about on your day for yourself. Is it really that important? You may say, "If I just had enough money, I'd be able to do whatever I want." But if you read about the people who have made great fortunes, you'll find that their passion for their business was much greater than their passion for money. They didn't make a lot of money because they loved money; they made money because they loved what they were doing. Again, imagine yourself having more money than you could possibly spend in a lifetime; imagine owning whatever you want right now. Then what? What happens after that? Even Bill Gates, whose passion for his business made him the Michael Jordan of computers, has decided that there's something else in his life that's more important.

Take Your Time—Make It *Your* Time

You'll find your mind wandering, of course, and on this day, you shouldn't force yourself too hard to stay on the subject. The subject is you, and you'll always be there, sometimes most of all when you least expect it. You're in this for the long haul.

However, if you start to think about the bills and the laundry, go back to your notebook. You're already well into some good work there. You can think about any one of the Ps, but for some it's easier to start with your priorities—they are what you want to get done first, the things that are closest to your heart, the things that you've probably thought about already.

Say you wrote down that you want to lose weight. Then you crossed that out and wrote, "I want to be a slender, healthy person," because by now you know that it's always better to think of things in a positive way. Now, being slender and healthy is a good thing, right? Not too many of us are going to write down, "I'd like to be so fat that at the diner I need two stools to sit on." So what's keeping you from that? Get real now. What exactly are the things that keep you from being slender and healthy? You might even want to separate that into two priorities—"I want to be slender" and "I want to be healthy." So how slender do you want to be? Skin and bone? Lean and mean? Just enough to fit into your old clothes?

Then think of all the ways you're going to get there: eating less, eating less often, eating different foods, exercising more, changing when you eat. Enjoy the idea that you can control your eating habits in a variety of different ways. In later chapters, I'll give you more tools to turn your collection of ideas into a focused, livable plan for the future.

Life is not a sprint, it's a marathon.

Thinking about your passions should be one of the most pleasurable parts of the day. If you're still having trouble feeling excited about something, it's probably because you've spent too much time working for other people's passions, or lost confidence in your abilities. Ask yourself what you would do if you could do anything and know you would be a success at it. When are the times you feel happy? If someone were going to give you all the financial support you needed, what business would you start? What new thing would you learn about? If you could do anything you wanted in the company of your best friend, what would it be? If you were to give yourself a special treat, what would it be? Where would you go? Remember, forget about making money or family responsibilities, or even aches and pains. Pay special attention to the things that you put a star next to when you were writing your list of wants. It often happens that you see the most when you are looking somewhere else.

Explore things that you would like to do but which seem absolutely out of the question. You may want to take a jet to a beach or explore the jungle—things you can't do on the spur of the moment. But make a note about them, the things that seem ridiculous or impossible—they may be the very things that you need to think about seriously. The other watchword for the day is: Anything is possible. If you can find your God idea, then you can make it happen, no matter how enormous it is. There are great things waiting to happen to you, things so wondrous that you can barely imagine them.

In the first chapter, I asked you to circle one of your wants—the one you would be willing to change your life for in order to make it come true. If it's something that you are truly committed to, it probably combines purpose, passions, and priorities. Now write down every reason why you can't have that want today, all the things that prevent you—money, family, time—and all the feelings that make you reluctant or resistant or downright discouraged. And don't worry, because I'll tell you about the next set of tools you'll need to overcome each and every one of those roadblocks on the highway of your success.

> *Faith is to believe what you do not yet see; the reward for this faith is to see what you believe.*
>
> —St. Augustine

It's been a long day, I'm sure. If you've done even most of the things I suggested, you've worked very hard. If you haven't, you've still accomplished more than you will in most workdays. As I said, I suspect that you will return to work tomorrow with a curious feeling of refreshment. You'll begin to look at what you're doing in new ways and perhaps see new ways to do it. In your head will be a new set of values and standards.

What you've done is to make that first step toward becoming a new person. You've planted a seed that will keep growing and greening. This day won't be the end of your work on finding your purpose and realizing your passion, but it will focus your thinking and make you more alert to those moments that will really be the defining ones in your life.

At the end of the day, there may be a dozen thoughts in your notebook, or only one. You may not have written anything down, and that may simply mean that you need to sleep on it. Or the dozen thoughts may really be only one, or the one thought might have a dozen parts. That is, you may not be at the end of your journey, but you will have taken the first step. Congratulations. You've started the journey that will change your life forever.

- Decide to take control of your life.
- Take time for yourself.
- Stop waiting for approval, start creating—your eternity is in your hands.

YOUR UTMOST LIVING JOURNAL

This chapter can make use of a great deal of the work you've already done, but here are some more questions that might help your mind start to spark.

What are your talents and abilities? What are the things people compliment you about? What are you most proud of when you've finished? What's the best thing about you?

What do you most enjoy doing?

What do you least enjoy doing?

_____

_____

_____

Write a brief autobiography of your utmost life. Remember, for this day, the sky's the limit.

_____

_____

_____

_____

_____

_____

_____

_____

What are the things you really, really want to do but don't think you'll ever be able to accomplish?

_____

_____

_____

What purpose would you like to try on for size tomorrow?

_____

_____

_____

5
. . .

Let the Feast Begin

Today you're going to start being the person you want to be. Today. Not tomorrow, not next week, but today. You've probably heard the phrase "Today is the first day of the rest of your life," but I don't want you to think of it that way. Today is the first day of *your life*. It's new and fresh, full of promise and hope, and it's time to make the most of it. It's a life you will control with confidence and gratitude. I don't want you to be living your life one day at a time. Today is the first day on your road to success.

You've already accomplished a great deal. You've begun to understand what you want to do (your purpose), what you can do to reach that goal (your passions), and how you want to do it (your priorities). You've begun to exercise your imagination so that it can show you where you are going and how to overcome the obstacles in your way. You've sharpened and focused the hunger that only the right meal for you can satisfy. Now it's time you put in your order.

Position Yourself for Utmost Living

The first step in taking control of your life is to use the work you've done envisioning your utmost life and start setting concrete goals for yourself. What if you woke up in the morning and said, "I don't know who I am and I don't know where I'm going, but I'm getting really, really mad because I'm not getting anywhere"? That's the way we are if we don't have goals.

> *A man without a purpose is like a ship without a rudder.*
>
> —Thomas Carlyle

If you've been working with me so far, you'll already have some ideas about what goals you want to set for yourself. In fact, you'll probably have several different kinds. There will be immediate goals and long-term goals. There will be goals that are a step to another goal, and goals that override everything else in your life. You may have goals in the personal, social, and financial dimensions of your world.

It can be a bit like a puzzle, if only because certainly some of these goals are related to one another. But as we work on them, I'll give you some ideas about how to put them in the order that will work the best for you. Always remember that this is about your life and your desires, not mine. You're making up your own personal menu.

For those of you who don't have one goal that calls to you, I'll give you some ideas about how to put your goals in an order that works for you. But ask yourself why there isn't a goal that stands out. Are you the kind of person who has a hard time making up your mind? Or are you someone whose mind changes from one day to the next about what seems important? Or perhaps when you start to think about a goal that really attracts you, it suddenly seems like too much effort.

If any of these feelings are stopping you, remember the key ingredients to success that we discussed in Chapter 3: imagination, focus, and courage. Let's apply them to this situation.

- Imagine your goals as clearly as you can. Maybe if none of your goals seems particularly strong, it's because you haven't really envisioned all the benefits and rewards you will gain from them. Maybe you should ask a friend or a relative for help.

- Focus on one of the goals. Certainly there is something you can be excited about, or you wouldn't have written it down. Remember, you're not going to change your whole life all at once, just one piece of it that you're dissatisfied with. And this won't be the last achievement of your life, so it doesn't have to be the one that's going to shake the world. You'll get to those later.

- Have the courage to commit yourself. You're not getting a measles shot—you're making your life a better place to live in. No matter what happens, you will feel better about yourself. I guarantee it. Really! When you commit yourself to improving your life, when you act according to your values rather than your chores, when you feel the excitement of a goal becoming real, you have already made your life a better place.

You might even decide that your first goal will be to improve your imagination, to increase your ability to focus, or to find the courage that's inside you, as it is in everybody. You can observe a lot just by watching, Yogi Berra once said in a somewhat different situation. But you can observe a lot about yourself if you watch how you feel and how you think at every stage of this process of change, and make that part of learning how to change.

You can also use what I call the eye-doctor technique. Maybe you have perfect vision, so I'll explain it to you. When you go to the doctor to get glasses, he puts a pair of peepholes surrounded by a big plastic armature in front of you. He dials a couple of lenses into place and has you look through it, then he flips one of the lenses to a different prescription and says, "Which one is better, this one or that one?" You tell him. Then he changes one of the lenses again and asks once more, "This one or that one?" And so you keep comparing one lens against another lens until you get exactly the right one.

You can do the same thing with your goals. Take the first one and the second one. Which one looks better? Once you've made a choice (and you can always make a choice), pair the winning goal with the next one on your list, and so on, until you have only one, or maybe two, that you want to try out.

---

*Goal-setting unleashes
unbelievable power.*

—Robert H. Schuller

If you're a sports fan, you could arrange your goals in a grid the way they do the teams for the NCAA basketball finals. Match them up into pairs and pick the winner from each pair, then match the winners up and choose between them again until you get to the champion.

Look for pictures and drawings and videos of the way you want to be, the way you want to look, the way you want to live. Pin them up where you will see them during the day. This is your dream board, your vision board, and it will help you keep focused and aware of what you're aiming at.

You might want to start with a goal that is high on your priority list, even if it's as basic as cleaning the closet or learning to play tennis. Don't dismiss small accomplishments, for they can lead to bigger ones. You might pick a goal that you could accomplish by, say, next week. Once you start accomplishing, you will gain confidence and look for greater and greater ways to succeed. Like everything else, winning can become a habit.

Focus on the Details

The first rule in goal setting is to be specific. That won't surprise you because you've already been exercising those muscles in exploring your purpose, your passions, and your priorities. You're already becoming stronger and more accomplished, and now you're ready to start your ascent. You have a clear idea of what your ultimate goal is and probably some of the other things you'll have to accomplish first.

> *God is in the details.*
>
> —Michelangelo

If you haven't already, do the exercise we worked on in the previous chapter. List all the obstacles that could prevent you from achieving that goal. Be honest with yourself and be realistic. If you're not, the only person you'll be fooling here is yourself. You say you want to get a better job, but you feel you have to dress better and you don't want to buy new clothes until you lose some weight. Come on now. Unless your goal is being a high-fashion model, that is just a string of excuses. You can get a better job *so that* you will have the confidence to lose weight and be able to afford better clothes. Are you thinking of these barriers because you're still fearful of changing?

Being realistic does not mean giving up on your purpose or not pursuing it at the highest level. Remember, tune in to the Anything Is Possible Network. It is only realistic to acknowledge that you have promise in you. There is a champion within you, because you are made in the image of God and He won't let you down.

Once you've eliminated the excuses and adjusted your goals to a realistic target, the remaining obstacles simply turn into your immediate goals. You don't know enough about music to start composing? Fine, take a course. You don't have enough time to start writing a novel? Make some. You don't have enough money to buy the boat of your dreams? Use your talents to earn more. You can do it. I said that I will be challenging you and that you will find yourself redefining who you are, in bigger or smaller ways. You're going to become the person who gets these things done, as in: "I'm not a person who spends that extra hour in bed in the morning. I get up and get something done."

Your inner compass is trying to lead you on a fantastic voyage.

You get *something* done. Not everything, but one thing. One of the mistakes that many of us make is to think that accomplishing a goal is a one-step maneuver. That couldn't be more wrong. Goals are multistep processes. Each step has the potential to lead you in new directions or take you to a new level of accomplishment. That may sound daunting, but each step you successfully complete provides a feeling of accomplishment and growing strength. You will find yourself looking forward to discovering new paths, and enjoying the way you can take control and take advantage of them.

What is happening here is that you are working to give birth to the desire God has placed within you. I like to say that you have become pregnant with God's dream seeds. You may plan this, or it may happen to you unexpectedly, since that is the way life is. You take time to know what is happening, to become intimate with these seeds, to commune with them through study and prayer. You will learn, just like a woman who reads *What to Expect When You're Expecting*. And there will be surprises and growth pains; giving birth is not without its difficulties, though there is joy in every moment. You will begin to stretch and grow, and sometimes you will feel awkward and difficult. But you will want that dream to be birthed—and it will find a way if you prepare and let it happen. Position yourself to receive, not to resist.

Suppose you're in a dead-end sales job, but you love clothes, you love talking about clothes with people, and you love putting people in the right clothes for them. You want to get to a place where you can do that all the time, and you decide that you will have the most chance to do that at the top. That's great.

Reaching the top in your company means becoming the director of merchandising. Now—realistically—you can't go directly from where you are to being director of merchandising. You need to focus in on how to get there by setting some intermediate goals. Work backward from where you want to be, step by step. The level below director of merchandising is store director. The level below that is department manager, and so on, down to the step right above where you are now. Your first goal is that next step.

Think about the tools and knowledge you'll need. Should you take classes? Do you need to meet people? Do you need to reorganize your time? Who can help you do this? Everything and everyone you know can be a resource in learning about it. Look within yourself, look outside yourself. Look for mentors, and don't be afraid to ask for help in finding people who can give you their experience and challenge you with their ideas. Just as iron sharpens iron, associating with other dreamers, world shakers, and history makers will help you reach your goals with greater ease.

Let's suppose that you've done your homework very well. You've studied, met people in executive merchandising jobs, and talked to them. In fact, you might be surprised at how welcoming and helpful these people were, but you've also discovered that the director of merchandising doesn't really spend a lot of time talking about how clothes look and how they look on people. That person spends a lot of time looking at Excel spreadsheets and yelling at the assistant directors and top managers. These are things you totally, totally hate to do, and in fact, since you've been honest about your priorities and passions, you know that you don't even want to become good at them.

You're stunned. You're at a loss. Now what?

Now you take even more advantage of all the work you've already done. You look at your passions and your purpose again, and you see that what you like is *talking* to people about their clothes and *finding great clothes for these people to wear.* Since you've done some research, you've heard about personal shopping, but you were kind of turned off because it was all about the store pushing the clothes that it needed to sell that season. It sounded kind of creepy to you, kind of underhanded, because you really wanted to help people, not just take their money. You're clear about your purpose.

Taking the Roof off Your Dreams

So you look at your passions again, and you do something absolutely crucial and wonderful: you take the roof off your dreams. You start to think big in small places, making yourself the biggest life you can think of. Too often we're trapped by our everyday responsibilities, the demands of a job, and the expectations of co-workers and friends. All these notions about what we can do and should do are like walls around us. They grow so high we can't see over them. We need to knock down those walls by asking questions such as "Why can't I do what I want to do? Who says it's not possible?" There is no limit to what's possible—that's simply the way the world was made. Your job is to take advantage of it.

So you make room for the big, like a family cleaning out their garage to make room for a new car. You decide that you are going to make a life out of talking to people about clothes in any store, any-where, and advising them on what they should wear whether it's what the stores are pushing that season or not. It is brilliant and it is wonder-ful because you have done the work you need to do in order to be brilliant and wonderful. You have trusted in your God idea more than other people's ideas or the boxes on the organization chart. You have taken the roof off your dreams and reached for the sky. And the sky will bend down to greet you.

You are so excited by the idea that you immediately begin to sketch in the details. You need to know selling; you need to know fashion; you need to know the stores; you need to know people who can afford to hire a personal fashion consultant.

You've just reached one of the most important steps, perhaps *the* most important one, in setting goals: you have made it real to yourself.

You can see yourself doing it. You watch someone wander through your department, and you think, *I know exactly what she needs to look gorgeous.* Your imagination and your focus give you the courage to walk over and strike up a conversation. The customer is wary at first—"I've really got to pick up my son at school"—yet you are so genuinely enthusiastic that she is quickly won over, especially when you take her to another department because the clothes there will fit her particular shape better. She has to leave to pick up her son, but she asks you for a card. No one has ever asked you for your name before, much less your card. You say you don't have one, but you'll be working at this time or that time and you'd be happy to talk to her again.

Things that matter most must never be at the mercy of things that matter least.

—Goethe

The customer leaves and you are tingling. You look around for someone else to help, and realize you're not in your department and had better get back there quick. But you want that feeling—of connection, of fulfillment, of fun and adventure—never to end. You will not be satisfied until that's what you can do all day, every day.

Congratulations. You have reached the level of divine desperation. But then you remember Tim's rules and get real specific about what you want and how to get there. Become store manager so that you know the best customers. Do the same thing at another store, and another. Working back, you see you will have to keep up with your city's sense of fashion—reading the newspaper, the local magazines. Wait, you'll have to get to know all the people who influence your city's taste, or at least a good chunk of them. And before that you'll have to learn about sales, and before that . . . You get the idea.

You'll get specific; you'll find out what you need to know; you'll envision the life you will be leading when you've become a successful personal shopper and spend your days doing the things you love and helping other people to look as good as they can—and to feel a little better about themselves because of it.

You've zeroed in on where you are going and why. Now we'll figure out when and how to measure your progress. As I said, you need to be specific. The first thing to do is to set milestones for yourself. Make your goals measurable. Otherwise you'll never be certain that you've achieved them. You need to know exactly where you're going. If you want to lose weight, decide how many pounds you want to weigh or what size dress you want to fit into. If you want to make more money, decide how much more every year for a specific number of years. If you want to learn to play the piano, figure out how many hours a week you can devote to practicing and taking courses.

Even if your goal is a creative one, such as learning to paint, you can determine how many hours a week you'll work on it. Not only that, you can set milestones, such as being part of a local art show, or being shown in a local gallery, or just finishing a work every three months. As you start to think in these terms, you'll be surprised at how precise and specific you can make your goals—because they are yours and yours alone. Although creative inspiration cannot be predicted, it can certainly be given a good kick in the pants. Great artists don't wait for inspiration to strike; they paint, write, or sing for a certain number of hours every day, and inspiration comes to them. If you try hard enough to find God, He will find you.

Another important aspect of specific milestones is when you are going to reach them. Zig Ziglar says that goals are "dreams with a deadline." What you are making, however, is your dateline, your lifeline, your liveline, the dates by which you live your utmost life. You decide you'll run a mile in under fifteen minutes *by this time next year.* You'll land a part in a prime-time television show *within five years.* Set a deadline for each intermediate step in your plan.

---

*Luck is a matter of preparation
meeting opportunity.*

—Oprah Winfrey

Again, you need to be realistic about these milestones and times. You have to feel challenged about reaching these goals. Both those words are important—your goal should be both realistic and something that will challenge you. Without that challenge, there will be no reward. If you set your goal as reading *War and Peace* within the next twenty years, you won't have any feeling of satisfaction when you get there. You may have forgotten the beginning by the time you reach the end. I always say that if you aim at nothing, you'll probably hit it. If you aim too low, you'll shoot yourself in the foot.

People generally have two reactions to setting goals that are so specific in terms of time and achievement. Some people can't get enough of it. A friend of mine wrote out all the goals that he intended to achieve in the next twenty years. He was clear and specific about each one and how he was going to pursue it. Now, five years later, he's already achieved more than half his goals.

Don't let setting goals become your goal, however—that's just another way of putting off goals. Suppose you find yourself planning relentlessly, refining the steps constantly, and readjusting your plans daily.

Stop and think—doesn't that tell you something? If you enjoy the planning more than the execution, you should include that in your thinking about your passions and your priorities. There are many great opportunities for someone who can write coherent, focused, useful plans. You may have a future in it. As you work your way through this banquet of your life, nothing is ever lost if you take the time to make use of it. Remember that God is everywhere in your life. He doesn't say, "Gotta go. Check back in with you next Wednesday." Everything you do is, effortlessly and effusively, an expression of your God idea.

But another reaction to specific, realistic, measurable goals is something we've seen before and will see again—fear. Suddenly the idea of changing—of achieving things that you had always thought were just dreams, of challenging yourself about something that you really care about—becomes real.

You will have to be the person who does those things. That's good; don't be upset by this fear, but learn to envision the future. You're beginning to understand that you can change your life—it's the reality that is making you afraid, so you've actually taken a step forward. Facing it and staying in touch with your purpose and your passions and accepting the fact that change will challenge you is one of the most crucial steps in the whole process. When you can really see it, you'll find that your eagerness to reach that future will start to overcome the fear.

MOTIVATION + FOCUS = COURAGE

Suppose you reach one of your goals—becoming an in-house sales manager. You've made every effort, you aced the interviews, you're confident that you can do the job, and one day the boss calls you into his office and congratulates you on your new position. You have a new office. You have an assistant. But suddenly all those good friendships you built up in the office are different. People who used to be your peers are now your subordinates. You have other subordinates who have been with the company longer than you have. Some of them start to complain about you. What do you do?

---

*Fear cannot be without hope, nor
hope without fear.*

—Benedict de Spinoza

Unfortunately, all too often people try to remain the person they were before. It never works. You can be a friendly boss, but you can't be a friend one moment and a boss the next. You have to learn new ways of relating to these people, and you have to face them to do it. You sit down with each of them individually and talk about your new relationship. You say that you will try to be fair, but you will also demand the best of them. They will appreciate the frankness, and you will be more comfortable with the many other new challenges you are facing.

If you don't learn to face your co-workers, to face up to your new job, and to face down the challenge of being a new you, you'll never accomplish anything. Don't rush yourself. Think about these goals for a few days. Revise them until you are comfortable. You may simply have challenged yourself with too much too quickly. But don't back down either; you want to change, and you can change.

This is all part of another crucial area of effective goal setting: preparing yourself mentally, physically, and emotionally to fully commit to your goals. You've already started to prepare yourself mentally by writing down your goals and making them specific, measurable, and realistic.

Think about what kind of life you will have when you have realized your goal. See yourself in your success. Think about that life in the present tense, as if you are already there and enjoying the fruits of your success. What do you look like? How are you dressed? Where are you living? What kind of people are you with? Paint it in rich colors and textures. Imagine the difficulties and challenges and think about how you will face them. Take your time—the more real you can make it, the sooner it will become reality, *your* reality.

Visualization can also help you avoid missteps and setbacks on the way to your goal. Suppose you've decided to quit smoking: you've decided when you are going to do it, what you will substitute in place of smoking, and how it will feel when you don't smoke anymore. You know there are certain times when it's hard to resist, certain situations that will let temptations slip in, certain people who will, without thinking, put you in a position to blow smoke into next week.

So when you work on envisioning yourself as a nonsmoker, think of those times. You know you're going to want a smoke after dinner. What are you going to do when that urge strikes? Take a walk? Call a friend? Have a Twinkie? Whatever it is, have it ready and pull it out of your pocket as soon as dinner is over. You know that there's an office party next Thursday that is really required for anyone who wants to move up in the company. You also know that if you sit around at a party, you are going to want a smoke. So what are you going to do? Explain politely that you've quit smoking. Have some chewing gum and a snack ready. Take a walk around the block. Maybe arrange ahead of time with the person organizing the party that there will be a smoking section and a nonsmoking section.

The point is that if you think ahead and visualize the future as clearly and in as much detail as possible, you will be able to make an end run around those temptations and weak moments. But you have to be prepared; you have to be ready with your alternative, with your substitute pleasure, even *before* that lurking temptation arises.

Imagine yourself waking up in the morning and thinking, *What will my life be like when I've reached my goal?* You remember my sister's friend, the Olympic medalist. She woke up every day knowing that she would spend four hours swimming. Are you OK with that kind of dedication? Suppose we go back to our personal shopper. She would spend time in clothing stores with her clients. Some of those clients would probably be difficult and demanding. There would probably be days when she was making just enough money to pay her bills. Would there be days when she was building spreadsheets and worrying about the numbers just like those merchandising directors? You bet. But the difference is she would be doing it so that she can do what she loves most.

Our personal shopper would have to be sure of herself and confident of her abilities—at least to her clients. She would need to work hard to find new clients, at least at the beginning. She would probably have times when she wondered why she had risked so much for this. Doubts assail everyone, but some people know how to respond and how to overcome doubt, worry, and uncertainty. She would make a list of her resources—ways she could find new business.

Finally, make sure that you are physically ready: rested, toned, eating right, exercising regularly. Make sure it won't be so stressful that you will tire and lose your concentration and focus. If you need to prepare in some way, build that into your plan.

Imagination, focus, and courage are the fuels for your fire, the steel that builds a house where your dreams can become real. Without them you don't have a chance of turning a wish into reality. From them are born the qualities we need to accomplish our purpose: motivation, persistence, determination, dedication. Nothing should be more important than achieving what you want. It's not about being selfish. On the way and when you get there, you'll most likely be helping someone else. Whom are you going to help sitting watching TV all day?

The one component that will make it happen is your total commitment to it.

When I first learned about these essential elements in achieving what I hoped to become, I felt overwhelmed. Very overwhelmed. *Over-overwhelmed.* I was setting goals that included years of schooling before I became an ordained minister. People who knew me thought I was crazy. They said, "Look at who he is and where he lives. He doesn't have a father." They said, "He's not going to make it. Who does Tim Storey think he is?"

Work is love made visible.

—Kahlil Gibran

It was not easy. It took a lot of years and a lot of effort. But I realized those goals. And I'm not special. Those people are shocked today. I became the person I wanted to be and found I had a whole page of new goals to set. Does that sound depressing? No, it's exciting; it's living an utmost life, it's having a God idea. When you achieve one goal, you have two or three more waiting in the wings as well as some old goals you haven't quite accomplished yet. Maybe they'll stay the same. Maybe you'll readjust them to fit new circumstances in your life. Your goals need to be flexible, but never give up on them.

The final step in effective goal setting is to make them public. Writing them down is an excellent way of doing it. It's like making a contract with yourself. As always, try to make the clauses of the contract as specific as possible. And you should keep a copy of your goals handy. Put them on a card that you can keep in your wallet or tuck in the corner of your mirror. Say your goal out loud to yourself. Say it like you mean it. In the morning, look in the mirror and say it again.

Ask yourself what can possibly keep you from your goal. Be alert for those moments. When one comes along, remind yourself of your goal. That will keep you focused.

Another way of making your goals public is by telling your friends, your family, everyone around you. Give them the details about what you're going to do and when. Make them a part of your dream, either as supporters or as partners. The more you talk about it to other people, the more real it will become.

Don't expect to get where you want to be in a day, a week, or even a year. But remember that every step you take will have a new liveliness to it; you will have new energy. Every level has levels in between, and each one has its own rewards.

- Set concrete goals.
- Be specific about how to accomplish those goals.
- Make your goals public—write them down, tell them to your friends and family.

YOUR UTMOST LIVING JOURNAL

1. The first step in transforming your life, of kicking your life up all the notches that you deserve, begins with visualizing exactly how it will feel when you are exercising your passions according to your priorities in accordance with your purpose. Describe how that will feel, what it will look like, who the people in your life will be, how you will balance your personal life and your work life. Savor it, make it real.

_____

_____

_____

Now double everything you hope to accomplish—just for starters.

2. Then start to write the recipe for your success. What are the ingredients? What are the tools, skills, knowledge, and relationships you will need to realize that utmost life? Don't worry about money, age, or anything else that makes you discouraged. If the idea *I can't do this because* . . . leaps into your head, turn that idea around: *I will be able to do this once I have* . . . If it helps you, pretend that you are writing this for someone else. Or write a résumé of who you will be when you've reached your goal. Try to think of someone who is doing or has done what you want to do, and try to find out how he or she got there.

_____

_____

3. Now look at each one of those steps toward your success and figure out how to make it part of your life. This is an exercise that will grow and develop along with your dream. If you come to something that you don't know how to obtain, work on why you don't know—again, do you need to learn a new skill, meet a new person, or save money? For each problem in your path, write down the solution.

_____

_____

_____

_____

_____

_____

6

. * .

You Have
Everything You Need

Now you're prepared. You have a goal, you know what you're doing and why. You have that picture painted in your head about what your life is going to look like. Next you need the tools and skills to get you there. Where are your paintbrushes—what you are going to use to paint the landscape of your life? What are the techniques? What do you have to learn now so that you can transform your life?

You know what? You already have everything you need.

Before you throw the book at the wall, let me add that although you already have everything you need, you may not have used your abilities regularly and consistently. The two things that you need are motivation and persistence. You don't need to be a genius. You don't need to have a special talent. You don't need to be able to bench-press four hundred pounds. But listen to this: if you use your motivation to persist in the pursuit of your dream, you can become a genius, you can develop special talents, and you can even bench-press four hundred pounds, if that's what you really want to do. And if you've been working with me and with your notebook, you've already been using those tools and building up those skills.

No one can go back and make a brand-new start, but anyone can start here and make a brand-new life.

—Anonymous

Let me tell you a story about an ordinary guy who has accomplished what might seem impossible. You've probably heard these kinds of stories before. But you haven't *heard* them; you haven't heard that *you* are the person in that story. You haven't realized that there is no difference between that person and you except that the person in the story has done what you're going to do. I want you to hear this story and imagine yourself inside of it. I want you to try to think what it took to take W. Mitchell where he has gone.

W. Mitchell (who prefers not to use his first name) lived in San Francisco, and he learned to fly a plane so he could appreciate those beautiful hills from a special vantage point. Then one day he was riding to work on a brand-new motorcycle, so he was being extra careful. But not everyone else was. A truck ran a red light and crashed right into him. The motorcycle burst into flames, and Mitchell was burned over 65 percent of his body. His fingers were burned off; his nose and ears were gone. It took sixteen operations before the doctors could re-create his face. But Mitchell would not let that stop him.

He moved to Colorado and began flying a plane again. He started a wood-burning stove company with a couple of friends. Then his light plane crashed and crushed twenty-two vertebrae in his back, paralyzing him from the waist down. But W. Mitchell believes with all his heart and soul that "it's not important what life does to you. What's important is what you do about it." He became the mayor of Crested Butte, Colorado. He ran for Congress with the slogan, "Not just another pretty face." He married and earned a master's degree in public administration. He eventually became an acclaimed public speaker and a millionaire. He never stopped to bemoan his fate. He never cursed his problems, or nursed them, or rehearsed them for his friends. He reversed them. He says that before he was paralyzed he could do ten thousand things. Now he can do nine thousand. He prefers to dwell on the nine thousand things he can do, not the one thousand that he can't. How did he do it? With the same gifts you've been given.

An oak tree is just an acorn that held its ground.

—Fred Shero

So let's stop and think about W. Mitchell. I'd be willing to bet that if we just look at the exterior, you're probably in better shape than he is. Yep, I'm pretty confident about that. So what did he have on the inside? Well, you say, it's obvious—he survived these terrible accidents. True enough. Do you think that gives him an advantage? Do you think you need to go through a terrible accident in order to achieve your heart's desire?

Adversity can do that sometimes—it can make you aware that you must be here for a purpose. I didn't tell you that W. Mitchell has a deep and strong faith, but I'm not asking you to put his accomplishments down to his faith. What I am asking is that you feel the same feeling—

that you are here to accomplish something. You may feel that something in your exterior or even your interior is scarred, not put together right, out of shape. So? That doesn't mean that you can't do everything you want to do. Whatever your failings or defects, you can overcome them. Get used to the idea. You remember what Captain Picard always said to his fellow crew members on the *Enterprise:* "Make it so." If you want something, you can make it so.

> *Everyone is necessarily the hero of his own life story.*
>
> —John Barth

Motivation and persistence are the gifts God gave everyone so that they could fulfill their promise. But as in so many things, He didn't make it a slam-dunk to master them. Everybody has motivation and persistence, and everybody can use them, but not everyone does when they should. That's what I'm here for.

Motivation is the kick that starts you going where you want to go. It gives you the strength to overcome the problems; it keeps you thinking optimistically; it keeps you up in a down world. Motivation is what says, "I really am going to attain these goals. This is my year to get out of debt." It keeps you from being intimidated, frustrated, or worn down.

Make a Date with Your Dreams

One of the masters of motivating people, Dale Carnegie, said that the only way to get someone else to do something is for them to *want* to do it. So what happens when *you* are the person you want to motivate? How can you make yourself want something? How do we get to the point of doing the hard work of changing ourselves? I mentioned divine desperation in Chapter 4. As you'll recall, the bad example of my uncles was the thing that opened my mind to changing my life, and the good example my sister gave me—her friend who won silver at the Olympics in swimming—helped me understand what would be necessary. Those were the things in my life that gave me the opportunity to feel that desperation.

My divine desperation motivated me to imagine what my utmost life would be like, but imagining that life is a way to engender that divine desperation. It's like chocolate—once you savor the taste of the future, there's no going back. You've been doing the same thing in the course of this book, if you've stayed with me. You have taken a look at your life and searched yourself for the hunger that will empower you to enjoy life to the utmost. You've singled out what you most want to change in yourself. You've imagined how it will look and feel to be that changed person. You've tasted in your mind just what that meal will be.

> *If one advances confidently in the direction of his dreams, and endeavors to live the life which he has imagined, he will meet with a success unexpected in common hours.*
>
> —Henry David Thoreau

How important is imagination? You'll be amazed at what it can do. The way we think determines how we act. It says in the Bible, "For as a man thinks within himself, so is he." Shakespeare wrote, "Nothing is but thinking makes it so." It's not just an opinion, it's a fact. When you center your thinking on an idea to the exclusion of everything else, that idea becomes a reality.

It's a power that works both ways. If your thoughts are filled with fear and worry, your life will be unstable, anxious, and insecure. If you think only of the bad things that can happen, the good things will pass you by. If you think you don't deserve to win, you'll never come in better than second. And you won't enjoy even that.

It's been said many times by many people, which only means that it's probably true:

> *Watch your thoughts, they become words.*
> *Watch your words, they become actions.*
> *Watch your actions, they become habits.*
> *Watch your habits, they become character.*
> *Watch your character, it becomes your destiny.*

We make our own reality. We make it every day in every way, sometimes when we don't even realize that's what we're doing. The reason I've been so insistent that you should imagine your ideal future, envision it in the smallest detail you can think of, is because the more vividly you can see it and the more attractive it is to you, the stronger its motivational power will be. You might call it willpower, and that's OK, but it's not a force that's pushing you; it's a power that you can control, and if you do, it will lead you in the direction you are aiming. You are in charge.

I've learned how effective imagination can be. I use it all the time now, even for things that seem wildly impossible, like finding a home for all the people on the streets of America, or solving the problem of street gangs in inner cities. I know that I may not accomplish every single thing that I imagine, but listen to this—I find that I come up with some idea that helps a little. A lot of the work we do with StoreyDreams Foundation came through this kind of dynamic thinking. When we started, we didn't have any idea that major corporations, star athletes, and celebrities would all come together to help us fight drugs, gangs, and other inner-city problems. But they did. So I say, go for it. Go for the gold, and don't be surprised when you get it.

> *The mind is the limit. As long*
> *as the mind can envision the fact*
> *that you can do something, you*
> *can do it. As long as you really*
> *believe 100 percent.*
>
> —Arnold Schwarzenegger

You may have attempted these exercises and decided that the whole project is hopeless. There are so many things to change and there's so much work to do that you don't have a prayer of reversing your behavior. I felt that way too for a while, but as my son learned in the first grade, the way to eat a hippopotamus is one bite at a time. Don't think you're going to change everything overnight. One bite at a time.

Taking Control of Your Subconscious Mind

There are some tricks that help keep that motivation up to the utmost level. Writing a contract with yourself is one. Keeping that card handy with your goal on it—and reading it—is another. Telling your family and friends what your plans are is another. All of these things are additional ways of changing the reality around you to make it conform to what you need in order to accomplish your goal.

Habit is habit, and not to be flung out of the window by any man, but coaxed downstairs one step at a time.

—Mark Twain

But the most important thing you can do is to get control of your subconscious. The other day I was having lunch with some of my friends. I'd made what I thought was a firm commitment to start eating a healthier diet. I'd backed up a little bit and eaten a couple of Twinkies, but I was OK with that; I wasn't going to let that bother me. I was going to cut down on eating sugars and fats and go back to the basics. I was pumped up about getting my body in shape and staying that way.

I sat down and my conscious mind said, *Tim, my boy, you're going to have the meat loaf, because it's made with turkey, which is much better for you than beef, and you're going to have a lemonade. It's a nourishing meal.* I let all my friends order first, and I was ready when the server turned to me. "I'll have," I announced, "spareribs and a large Pepsi." Even I was surprised. I hadn't even thought about eating spareribs until that exact moment. Listen to that: spareribs and a large Pepsi.

What went wrong here? Obviously, my subconscious had not gotten with the program, so there I was with a bib around my neck and barbecue sauce dripping down my arm. It was a lesson for me. It's easy to look at life's menu and decide what would be the best you can imagine. But then when it's time to actually do something about it, you fall back on the usual, the regular, the comfortable. It may not be good for you, it may not be what you really want, it may do you more harm than good, but there you sit with it on your plate.

Now, when I'm talking about ribs, I'm talking about a comfort zone for me. I grew up on ribs, my whole family ate ribs, and some of my best meals with my family were around ribs. Ribs are kind of my default food. Our subconscious doesn't mind that default food—or a default life. The subconscious can't really read the menu; it doesn't know what the other choices are unless it has already tried them. It's not capable of desiring change and has a very narrow field of vision.

Maybe that's why it's so powerful; it doesn't have to consider any alternatives. You have to trick it into a new idea. But on the other hand, precisely because it doesn't like change, once you've reprogrammed it into a new mode it will tend to stay that way.

A couple of things about the subconscious. First, it's a little hard of hearing. You can't just say something in your head and expect your subconscious to hear it. In fact, even whispering something doesn't work all that well, because your subconscious isn't sure that you mean it. No, you have to say it loud and say it proud.

It's important for you to *hear* it. Try it. Think of some task you've been putting off—cleaning out the closet, giving the dog a bath, or taking the kids out for ice cream. Say what you're going to accomplish aloud, firmly. Say it again, and this time say it like you really mean it. Get used to using our recommended daily vitamins—make a date, be specific, and be positive. Tell yourself what time you're going to do it and what time you're going to stop. Write yourself a note and put it in your pocket. If you have family, bring them into the project; tell them, "At four o'clock we're going to clean out the closet and make it look beautiful. Maybe there's hidden treasure there." See what happens.

Frequently, taking some real action can be a help. It's no accident that people who are really ready to quit smoking throw their last pack away. Probably they should throw each cigarette away individually. It's something to keep in mind, because we can't spend every waking moment on whatever goal we've set, however much we might think about it. For instance, if you are excited about looking slender and healthy, go to your pantry and throw out all the sweets and treats there. When you find yourself resisting—"I'll just keep this for those times when I have a real craving"—that's the item to throw away especially.

> *Identify what's holding you back from being great. Then go out and work on turning your weaknesses into strengths.*
>
> —Terry Bradshaw

Sure, there will be times when you have that snack, but make it harder for yourself to get it. That will also give you more time to reconsider. If your goal is becoming healthier, find a way to squeeze a little walk into your day. Even if you can't get outside, you can do the stairs in your building. There's nothing better for your heart, not to mention your waistline. Of course, all these techniques apply to personal, mental, and emotional goals.

The only trick to talking to your subconscious is that everything you say has to be phrased in a positive way. As I said, our subconscious mind is hard of hearing, so you have to say it in a way that can't be misinterpreted, misunderstood, or mismanaged. Your subconscious is a terrible manager.

Your subconscious loves it when you complain—when you say you're too fat or too old or tired of this or bored with that. So if you want to lose weight, don't say to yourself, "Gee, I'm going to lose some weight so that I don't look so fat and feel so sluggish." All your subconscious is going to hear is "fat" and "sluggish." It will work hard to fulfill that thought, that habit, that destiny. It's used to you being fat and sluggish, and it has become perfectly comfortable with that state and everything that took you there.

Instead, say proudly, "I'm going to become fit, strong, and healthy. When I lose fifteen pounds I'll look terrific and I'll have energy all day long." Imagine yourself at that new weight and don't think about how you used to look. Program your subconscious to whisper words of encouragement.

There's a sign that I see sometimes: MAKE SURE YOUR BRAIN IS IN GEAR BEFORE YOU PUT YOUR MOUTH IN MOTION. Make sure your subconscious understands what your conscious mind wants and is ready to help. And if you make a mistake and order the wrong thing, send it back as soon as possible—"I really want that turkey meat loaf"—and get back on the good diet. Think about how you're going to look and feel. Make a date with happiness, be specific, and believe.

Persistence Breaks Resistance

Persistence is the quality that takes the long view and applies it to the world. Persistence is what keeps us from failing because it's what keeps us from giving up. Everybody needs that. Persistence is what keeps you on course for your goal when there's opposition to your path, when there are obstacles. Calvin Coolidge said, "Nothing can take the place of persistence. Talent will not; nothing is more common than unsuccessful men with talent. Genius will not; unrewarded genius is almost a proverb. Education will not; the world is full of educated derelicts. Persistence and determination alone are omnipotent."

When you were a child and wanted to learn how to ride a bike, you didn't let falling stop you. First you figured out how to avoid hurting yourself in the fall, and then you just kept getting back on the bike. Until it became easy.

Then a few years later, you learned to drive. You were a lot more self-conscious, and didn't want to fail at this first really adult thing they were going to allow you to do. You didn't want to look stupid and knock over any of those orange cones they put around the driving course to tell you when you were off the track. Those cones looked huge. But you did your best and finally learned to drive. When you're a kid, you have the best motivation of all: you want to change your life. You want to grow up, become an adult, and do all the things that an adult can do. All ten thousand of them. You're always saying, "When I grow up, I'm going to . . ." or "When I'm an adult I won't have to . . ." You'll do anything—even some things you know are stupid—in order to get to the promised land of adulthood.

So what happens? We grow up and we grow supposedly wiser, and we suddenly stop trying. Our subconscious says it's all right if you don't have what you want. It becomes a seductive voice whispering in our ear, promising that everything is fine just the way it is. But this subconscious voice can be programmed to whisper encouragements, to make you stronger and keep you working against all odds.

Success is the sum of small efforts,
repeated day in and day out.

—Robert Collier

Persistence is the steel in the backbone that tells you that just because you haven't succeeded yet, you will as long as you keep trying. Persistence is the live wire that supplies the energy. Persistence is the knowledge that the world is not going to roll out the red carpet for you. You're the one who has to roll it out.

You remember that I had decided to change my life. In my heart there was a desire to help people, to make their lives better. So the first thing I had to do was to investigate. I asked myself, "What can I do with my life, my skills, my attitudes to help other people?" I had to look over the menu of life's choices to find the meal that was right for me.

By then I was at a community college in Fullerton, California. And one day I walked by a booth on campus for the Peace Corps. I still had my investigating hat on, so I went up to the booth and dialogued a little with the nice people there. One of the programs involved going to South America for the summer to help people. I started to get excited. *Wow, this is starting to make sense. I want to go and help change people's lives, and that's exactly what the Peace Corps is all about.* Here was a chance to go to foreign countries and bring relief to people. It began to feel right to me, so I took home some forms they gave me to fill out.

I looked over the forms and started to get a little worried. They kept asking about skills. Was I a plumber? Was I an electrician? My faith was beginning to wane. Just about the only skill I had in my toolbox was the gift of gab.

I went back to the Peace Corps booth, and a gentleman there looked over my forms and sort of smiled. "Have you ever done any construction work?" he asked. "Do you know anything about building a home?" I kept having to say no, there just wasn't much that I brought to the table. I walked away slowly that afternoon, thinking maybe this work was not for me.

But I had that God idea in me and it wouldn't let me go. At that point I didn't have the right tools and skills for the Peace Corps. Or for much of anything else, for that matter. But I had the right attitude. I persisted. I kept on investigating. I began reading about people who had succeeded in the ways I wanted to succeed. I read about Nelson Mandela, and that made a big impression. I'm not saying that I wanted to become Nelson Mandela; I just figured that I could do the things he did. The more I read about people like Nelson Mandela, the more helping people seemed the right choice for me. So I started to navigate myself into the right place to do that. I decided to go to seminary, learn biblical principles, and then go into social work.

The majority of men meet with failure, because of their lack of persistence in creating new plans to take the place of those which fail.

—Napoleon Hill

I didn't give up, and I feel that it was the right choice. One afternoon a long time after that dismal afternoon at the Peace Corps booth, I had lunch with Bobby Shriver, the son of the first director of the Peace Corps, Sergeant Shriver. He got a laugh out of the idea that Tim Storey had no gifts to offer the Peace Corps.

Have Faith in Yourself

So many people I know get right to the point of breaking through in life but then begin to cower; they lose their drive and their confidence. They think they need some magic formula that will make them succeed, and don't realize that persistence is the magic formula. As Woody Allen said, "Ninety percent of life is just showing up." Joking aside, he's saying that when you show up, you are there to take advantage of the opportunities. When you hit the wall, you weaken it. When you knock on doors and keep knocking on them, pretty soon opportunity starts to knock back. Persistence overcomes resistance.

Colonel Sanders went to more than a thousand people asking for a loan to start one of the most successful businesses in America. He knocked on a door and the answer was no, but he knocked on another door, and another and another, and at one of them the answer was yes. And he knocked on another door and he got another yes. And another. And another. It didn't take genius, though he may have been a genius. It didn't take education, and it certainly didn't take wealth. It took persistence.

If you only knock long enough and loud enough at the gate, you are sure to wake up somebody.

—Henry Wadsworth Longfellow

How do you get persistence? Is it like getting motivation? Do you have to convince your subconscious? Well, that doesn't hurt; motivation will build up your persistence. If you say to yourself at the beginning that you are going to accomplish your goal no matter what other people say, no matter what obstacles arise in front of you, you will continue. And you will savor overcoming the obstacles and proving the naysayers wrong, step by step, door by door.

Investigation will build up your persistence. The more you learn and understand about what you're trying to do, the more right it will feel to you. If it's your God idea, it will become like a magnet, drawing you to it so hard that you can't stop, won't stop.

And persistence is faith. Faith in yourself, faith in the miracle within you. Persistence is saying that no matter how many people say you're wrong, you're going to make it right. The Bible says, "Trust in the Lord with all your heart. Do not lean on your own understanding. But in all your ways acknowledge Him and He shall direct your path." It's really just saying that once you've seen what life is right for you, do not let others stand in your way. Do not let them steal your dreams. If the door slams in your face, knock on it a little harder. Or knock on a different door. Persistence is a faith in yourself that you and only you know what's right for *you.*

Chapter 2 of the gospel of Mark tells the story of a paralyzed man. Lying on his cot, he hears that Jesus is having a healing service and he wants to go. So four men carry this guy to the house where Jesus is healing. But when they get there, it's so crowded that they cannot get in through the front door. It's so crowded that they can't even see Jesus. But of course they know He's there.

They could have walked away. Had even one of the four left, it would have caused problems. But no one leaves. They all pick up the man and take him around to the back door of the house, but that's crowded too. So they climb onto the roof of the house, because back then houses had a hole in the roof. Sometimes people would get some fresh air by climbing out onto the roof of their house.

So now they're on the roof, but the hole is too small to get the man through. At least now they can see their goal, they can see Jesus. They have a paralyzed man on the roof of a house—they've come that far—and they can see Jesus, so they are not backing down. They begin to tear the tiles off the roof of the house.

Sometimes you have to do something you've never done before to get somewhere you've never been before. Those men didn't wake up thinking, *Oh, I think I'll carry a paralyzed man up to the roof of a house.*

They didn't expect to find themselves tearing tiles off the roof of a house. But they didn't stop; they didn't quit; they didn't give up. They had faith.

Jesus looked up and saw the faith of all five men. He saw their faith in their actions. Faith has a posture and an attitude. He sees their faith and the tiles flying off the roof and he lets them into the house, saying "Your faith has made you whole." And the man got up and walked. Persistence overcomes resistance.

We've talked about habits before, but it's at this point that you will really start to look closely at your habits and begin to transform them. Like the subconscious mind, habits can be a real snare for the unwary. The experts tell us that it takes twenty-one days to establish a new habit. Now, on one hand, twenty-one days doesn't sound like a long time, and it isn't, when you look at your life in the long view. It doesn't seem hard to substitute a healthy cereal for your usual cream cheese Danish for breakfast, or put aside an hour every other day to take a brisk walk, or read for half an hour before you go to sleep.

Every habit, good or bad, is acquired and learned in the same way—by finding that it is a means of satisfaction.

—Juliene Berk

But when you think about it, creating or changing a habit demands all the techniques we've been talking about in this book. One day you're out of cereal, so you can't eat it until you get to the store. The next day you've bought cereal, but you're late for work. *Oh,* you think, *it will be faster if I just stop by the diner and get a quick cup of coffee—and a cream cheese Danish.* Or you plan to take that walk, but the first day it rains. The second day, your son has a birthday party to go to just when you were planning to go out. The third day, you're just too tired because you had to stay up later doing the chores that you didn't get done the day before. And when you lie down to read that book, you fall asleep.

So making a habit takes foresight, preparation, planning, focus, and courage. Look ahead to what's happening this week. What will you need and when will you need it if you're going to change a habit? What are the things that could prevent you from doing what you've planned, and how are you going to avoid them? What other time do you have that you can substitute? What should you avoid doing, such as staying up late, so that you can do what you've planned, such as reading for half an hour?

It's easier to make a habit than to break a habit. Substituting cereal for your Danish is a habit that's easier to establish than simply not eating at all, especially not eating at mealtime. After all, eating breakfast is a habit that most of us have been accustomed to all our lives. It might even take more than twenty-one days to change a habit that ingrained. But perhaps you can substitute that walk for the snack you usually have in the afternoon. If it's raining then, you can do exercises in your living room or walk the stairs in your building. It's surprising how much time you can find if you look for it. The head of a great newspaper chain once compared time to a box full of tennis balls. In between the tennis balls, there was room for some jobs that were the size of golf balls. In between the golf balls, there was room for some jobs that were the size of marbles. There are almost always a few golf balls or marbles rolling around in your life.

Also, be aware of the habits that you don't recognize as habits. You may not realize that you have a pint of ice cream every time you get off the phone with your mother, but stop and think about it. Maybe you can substitute something for the ice cream—or phone your mother when you're in the middle of a traffic jam. There might even be times when you don't pick up the phone when your mother is likely to be calling. Remember, you can change the spaces, places, and faces in your life. Even with a face you love, you might need to put it in a different place. After all, it may be that your mother hasn't realized that her daughter is in a different place than she was when she was six years old.

Will it be hard? Yes. Will there be times you want to give up? Yes. Will there be times you do give up? Yes. But then you'll come back, you'll step up and step out, because you are motivated and persistent.

- Your imagination can create motivation and persistence.
- Don't let your subconscious take over when you're not watching.
- Decide to succeed and don't quit until you do.

YOUR UTMOST LIVING JOURNAL
Guidelines for Successful Goal Setting

1. Make your goals specific. The more defined your goals, the better your chance of achieving them.
2. Make your goals believable. They should fit with who you are and what your capabilities are.
3. Make your goals measurable. They should be well defined and qualifiable.
4. Give your goals a target date that is realistic. Every goal needs a deadline that defines it.
5. Envision your goals before they happen. By imagining how wonderful the reality is going to be, your subconscious helps you achieve it sooner.

6. Write a contract with yourself to accomplish your goals. For example:

A. I commit myself to becoming a successful chef in a restaurant by June 1, 2012. Nothing will keep me from accomplishing this goal. In order to do so, I will take classes in X, Y, and Z in the next two years. I will afford these classes by reducing my monthly expenses by $50 a month for the next year.

B. I will find a local caterer who will hire me if I have successfully completed the first class. Then I will start working on the weekends for this caterer, which will enable me to afford the next classes.

C. Over the next two years, I will find a job in a good restaurant that will enable me to quit my current dead-end job. I will have to be careful with my expenses, but because restaurant work has flexible hours, I can continue to work for the caterer and to take classes.

D. At the end of five years, I will have enough background and experience to apply for the position of line cook at X restaurant in the city, or its equivalent.

SIGNED: _____

Your contract may be more detailed than this one, but it should not be less detailed. The more positive steps you can build into it, the more you feel that you are accomplishing something every day, every week, every month.

7. Keep your description of your utmost life handy, and read it once a day. Add to it and refine it as you learn more and accomplish more.

8. Make preparations mentally, emotionally, and physically to fully commit to your goals. It takes commitment, dedication, and focus to turn a wish into a reality.

9. Keep a record of your accomplishments, and give yourself a specific reward, one that you determine ahead of time, when you achieve each one.

10. Revise the contract as necessary if you find that there are steps you didn't envision. But never break your commitment to yourself.

7

. . .

Your Support System

Wₑ've spent a great deal of time talking about how you can determine your purpose and passions, and how you can plan for and execute change in your life. But mostly we've been talking about working on yourself, and no life is lived in isolation. "No man is an island," wrote John Donne at a time when writers didn't always pay attention to gender, "entire of itself." We often hear the first part of that quote, but we sometimes forget to pay attention to the second part.

Of course we are all in the midst of a sea of people, but it is the relationships we have with those people that will determine the fullness and breadth of our lives. We can exist alone, but we won't be living a complete life. "Entire of itself," Donne wrote, which means to me that we are not whole, we are not complete, we are not entirely ourselves without other people in our lives.

Of course there are extremes in both directions—too much or too little human contact. I'm sure you know someone, maybe an older person, who has gradually shut out the rest of the world. A person who sees only the people who sell them food, or gasoline, or movies. Such a person speaks rarely to neighbors and doesn't go out to see friends. We think of these people, even when we love them very much, as growing smaller. That's not what you want.

Then there are those people who always seem to be going somewhere to do something with other people. If they have children, it's a PTA meeting, a meeting at school about their child, a soccer game, and maybe they also are going to a book group, going bowling, and going out for a few hours after work. In other words, it's always something. Some of these people complain that they have no real friends, or that people are always disappointing them, or that there's never anyone to help them when they need it.

There is an important difference between a filled-up life and a fulfilled life. If you're just filling up your life with people, acquiring them the way some people collect stamps or model cars, then you are cluttering your life. If you talk at them and if you don't hear them when they talk, you are as isolated as if you were alone all the time. You can be an island in an archipelago.

> *Real listening is a willingness to let the other person change you.*
>
> —Alan Alda

Truly being a part of the world always involves an exchange. I give to you and you give to me. We may exchange the same thing—information, techniques, contacts, ideas. Or we may exchange different things—I might give you an idea, and you will give me your enthusiasm for that idea. I might share a difficult and troubling problem with you, and you give me your support and sympathy. But the point is that there is a real exchange, and that means that there is a change—a change in me and a change in you. I gain something and you gain something. I think differently, or I feel different, or I act differently. You gain insight from my idea, and I gain energy from your enthusiasm. I gain strength from your compassion, and you gain the satisfaction of helping. This is an exchange where we both gain—we both keep the change.

So when we set sail in this sea of people, we want to hail other ships and exchange our news and goods, information and insight, and even friendship and love. But beware that there are also pirates. These are the people who want to gain without giving, and they come in many forms. They may seem friendly and exciting on the outside, or they may simply offer something that seems valuable. But their friendship turns out to be a one-way street, in which they take from us—our time, our care, even our money—and give nothing in return. Or what they offer turns out to be a sham. Nothing in them changes; their change is worthless.

I know what this is like. As you might imagine, I'm a pretty open kind of guy, but I've learned the hard way that not everyone is worth your time and generosity, even when they seem friendly and enthusiastic.

You will also know people who make your life difficult but are sincerely and consciously trying to help you. We probably all feel that way a little bit about our parents, at least some of the time. Our parents are always there to support us and love us, but they are also there to teach us limits and rules. That's not always a guidance that we immediately accept, but in the end, we usually see its importance. God works the same way in your life. He is there to guide you, but He is also there to goad you and to govern you. He will make changes in your life that you don't expect, changes that you don't feel ready for. But they are changes that He knows you need to make. And He doesn't always make it easy.

Getting Away from People Who Don't Get You

There will always be an opposition to your mission, and sometimes that opposition will take the form of someone who seems to have been born to make your life impossible. It might be your boss, or it might be a co-worker. It might be someone you consider a friend. It might even be someone in your family.

David knew about that. You remember David, the one who killed Goliath. But even before that, David had found favor with the Lord, and when God asked him to slay the giant, well, that was the last straw for David's brother Eliab. Eliab started a whispering campaign to discredit David, to make David's motives seem suspect, and to break up the good thing David had going with God.

It happens all the time. Just because you are starting to get right, because you are starting to achieve the goals you want, because you are standing taller, somebody will try to mow you down. Jealousy and envy are next-door neighbors and are always talking over the back fence. Jealous people are resentful of what you've accomplished, envious of your success. Frequently they are afraid that they will be the losers if you are a winner. They want to deprive you of what you've gained or take away the things you find gratifying and satisfying. They are resentful and malicious, suspicious and bitter.

Such people may start to whisper about you behind your back, causing others to doubt you. Like Eliab, they may spread rumors about your true motives and disrupt relationships that you have built up among friends and colleagues. Jealous people do not "get you." They don't understand that you have a plan and a purpose that are not related to them. They may be envious that you have a plan at all. But just as often, they don't even know why they are out to get you. That doesn't make them any less destructive to your mission.

Throughout history, jealousy and envy have started wars, broken families and relationships, and halted destinies. Of course the poster child for jealousy and envy in the Bible is Lucifer, and I'm sure you've sometimes felt as though you were fighting the devil when someone like that starts to work against you.

Tell me what company you keep and I'll tell you what you are.

—Miguel de Cervantes

The great danger is that your opposition begins to make you doubt yourself. That is when your God idea comes to your aid. If you know your purpose and know that it is for the benefit of everyone, then you will not be shaken in your faith. David knew that his intentions were pure, so he ignored his brother. He realized that his brother was speaking from his own problems, not David's. So David walked away from his brother and went to fight Goliath. He did not leave his priority pathway, and he accomplished his destiny. Remember, your purpose is the big idea; it is the reason for everything you do. You may have passions for one thing or another, and you may have plans to accomplish one thing or another, but your purpose is the reason that you are here on earth. As long as that is for good, and as long as your passions and plans are in harmony with that purpose, then you know that you cannot be doing wrong.

The Four Armors Against Jealousy and Envy

Along with the power of your God idea, you can protect yourself against jealousy and envy with four kinds of armor. They will take some courage to put on, but they will stand you in good stead.

The first armor is fairness. If you hear that someone has said something malicious about you, take a deep breath and try to take a fair and empathetic view of the situation. The person may be having a bad day, or be under a great deal of pressure, or have some kind of difficulty in their own life that is making them short-tempered and unreasonable.

The second armor is firmness. You must stick to your purpose and your passions. You must determine your boundaries as to what you will and will not allow. You may have to confront your tormentor, but that is not always necessary. Sometimes it is more effective simply to keep to your plan. The important thing is not to let anyone mess with your destiny. If you cannot reason with the person and he or she does not respect your boundaries, then maybe a friendship has to end. If it is happening at work, you may have to let others know about the problem and make it plain that you have no animosity against the person, but that you cannot allow lies to be accepted.

What is crucial is to turn your back on payback; the third armor is to shun revenge. At the very least, it wastes time that you could be using for your passions and plans. Most important, though, taking revenge thwarts your purpose. It can only sow seeds of more envy and jealousy, more attacks and responses, more pain and heartbreak. Stay clear of anything that can be seen as vengeance.

The fourth armor is keeping your own counsel. As we go through life we learn that we cannot confide in everyone. We learn that it is best simply to steer clear of some people. The Bible says, "A fool tells his whole heart," so we should avoid saying everything we know or feel to everyone in our life. There are those who cannot be trusted with it, and they can't stab you in the back if you don't let them on the inside.

---

*Staying even is better
than getting even.*

—Joan Lunden

Dining alone is no fun and it's not good for you. But just as your purpose will guide you about the places and spaces in your life, it can guide you about the faces.

Love and Friendship

No life can be full without family and friends who give you support and strength, love and lift. I was at a birthday party one time for one of Smokey Robinson's children. Smokey was barbecuing, and Leon Isaac Kennedy and I were talking to him. I asked Smokey, "What's the best thing about being Smokey Robinson?" Now of course this is a man who's received just about every honor the music world can give. He could have talked about recording "Tears of a Clown," or the old Motown days, or a hundred other things. But Smokey just smiled, spread his arms toward his kids and the party, and said, "The best thing is this." The best thing is friends and family.

Your family are the people who know you and know where you came from better than anyone else. They may make you gnash your teeth from time to time, but they will also give you some truth to chew over. Children often complain that their parents don't see them as adults, and that is often true, but it's also true that children don't insist that their parents see them as adults. Besides, how many of us want our mother or our father to treat us the same as someone who walks in off the street?

> *Call it a clan, call it a network, call it a tribe, call it a family. Whatever you call it, whoever you are, you need one.*
>
> —Jane Howard

The family you make for yourself is the family that will support you into the future, and each member deserves your respect just as you deserve theirs. A life without family is a life that pinches and blisters the soul. Our idea of family is very broad today—but it all comes down to creating a personal house that will provide shelter, respect, and security for the people you love. That respect means that you tell them what you are feeling and needing just as you listen to what they are feeling and needing. We're all responsible for the effect we have on the people around us.

Friendship is a special case of family. Good friends are people who can admire your accomplishments and also care enough to be honest with you. They are people who can challenge you and can offer you new vistas, who have a curiosity about life and enjoyment of it. Friendships can be a breath of fresh air in your personal world and can give you a perspective on your life—even your family—that can lead you to new insight and renewed enjoyment.

All that goes to show that love is a central part of an utmost life. And not just love, but loving and being loved. Leo Buscaglia, who has written beautifully about love, points out that the first person you have to love is yourself. However, that love is not an ego trip or a fantasy. It is based on reality. The person who loves himself or herself sees himself with accuracy and appreciates what is there—but can be excited and challenged by the prospect of what he or she can become. If you do not love yourself, you cannot truly accept love from someone else. You'll feel that you don't deserve it. If you think you're ugly, if you're down on yourself, you won't be able to accept that another person can truly love you. What's more, you won't be able to truly love someone else. After all, such a person thinks, *I'm such a bad human being that my love wouldn't be worth anything to anyone else.* Love of another is a reflection of how you feel about yourself.

With that kind of love you have the wealth to give love and accept love from other people, to share your love with others, and to believe that God loves you without measure. I believe that no life is truly fulfilled until it includes others and gives to them. We'll talk about this more later as we explore the utmost life.

The One, the Few, the Many, and the Multitudes

Jesus's life is a model about how to treat other people—whom to confide in and whom to treat with respect but distance. He did not share his heart with everyone. The Bible tells us not to "cast your pearls before swine, lest they trample them under their feet and turn and tear you into pieces" (Matthew 7:6). In concentric circles around him, Jesus had the One, the Three, the Twelve, the Seventy, and the multitude (in the Bible, the Five Hundred). With his Father, the One, he shared his whole heart. God is the one person you can absolutely depend on, and you'll be a whole lot better off if you do share your whole heart with God. Once you have shared the burden of fulfilling your destiny with God, you will find that you feel lighter and freer, stronger and more purposeful.

You may also have someone in your life with whom you can share all the burdens and successes of everyday life, all your hopes and your fears. A friend of mine told me a wonderful story about his five-year-old daughter. She would occasionally wake up in the middle of the night, and of course she was afraid. My friend and his wife had read all the books about raising children, so they didn't want to go to her right away—they wanted her to learn how to put herself back to sleep. So they would say to the little girl, "Don't worry, honey, we're close and Jesus is always watching over you." Then one night the little girl responded, "I know Jesus is always watching, but tonight I want somebody with some skin on!" All of us need somebody with some skin on to share our lives with in a loving and supportive relationship. Real love, which demands mutual fairness, honor, and respect is a blessing and a model.

Have no friends not equal to yourself.

—Confucius

Jesus also shared deeply of his soul with the Three—Peter, James, and John. Their relationship was a partnership of the spirit, and He knew He could depend on them as they depended on Him. He also knew that they were human and could make mistakes. He knew Peter would deny Him, and he forgave him that even before it happened. So it is with our closest partners and friends. What they give to us immeasurably repays the times that they slip.

And so on with the Twelve, the Apostles. These are people who share your life and help you through it without necessarily being with you at every step. They are close friends and family, people who pick you up when you are down, keep you warm when you are cold, and cover your back when you are too weak to do it yourself. They will celebrate your victories with you and help you back from your setbacks. Friendships are like a fine wine—they grow better with age. They should be carefully created and nourished.

If I speak in the tongues of men and of angels, but have not love, I am only a resounding gong or a clanging cymbal.

—I Corinthians 13

In the larger circles of people around you in your life, you will find many who will help you, who will guide you, who will make your life better. In these circles, there will be many different kinds of relationships. Some people are like a good snack. They are not demanding, but they are not fulfilling either. Some are friends for a day, some for a season, some for a lifetime.

I used to meet regularly at the home of Charlie Sheen with some other actors and friends of ours. That was a time when Charlie was going through some rough spots, but he was always optimistic and always trying to help his friends when they were going through their own troubles. It was amazing to see what a terrific caretaker he was of other actors who were facing challenges. He encouraged them by telling them that life goes on and that they could make it if they lived by design and not by default. So it was great to see Charlie keep fighting and eventually have such a huge success with *Two and a Half Men*.

Look for the mentors in your life, the people like Charlie who can teach you what you are looking for. There are many different kinds of mentors. Sometimes they will teach you directly, and other times they will give you the opportunity to learn. Assisting someone who has the job that you want is an example of that, and I profited from working with a motivational minister for several years. I traveled around the world with him, doing everything that he needed done. So I learned things from the ground up. I would do things like take care of the soundboard when he was speaking at an event. I handled the product table. I learned about organizing someone else's schedule and keeping everything in order. I learned to pay attention to detail. So years later, when I was speaking in Stockholm before eight thousand people, I could tell what was wrong with the sound system.

Some people can help you with something you need to learn or do or be. You may not have been looking for it, but they come into your life because it's the right time. At college there were very few people who were like me. I didn't feel comfortable there, and I was lonely all the time, but there were still people there to teach me. There was a man named Larry who taught me a great deal about Bible principles. He wasn't someone I would have spent a lot of time with in some other situation, but I saw the real strength he had. My friend Dan had a rich prayer life. We used to go into the piano practice rooms after hours and pray.

Teamwork makes a dream work.

—Ciara

You won't necessarily think of each of these people as mentors, but that doesn't mean they don't have something to teach you. My roommate, for instance, taught me how to be organized. I was a pretty average kind of guy when it came to neatness and cleaning up after myself. My roommate would walk in the room and say amiably, "Tim, do you really need your pants on the floor?" You see what I mean? But he taught me that it is just as easy to be organized as to be a slob—in fact, it's easier when you add up all the time I spent looking for things in that clutter. Not only that, I learned that I felt better about myself when I kept things neat and organized. I realized what it felt like to be on top of things.

The Partners in Your Dream

As you become committed to improving your life and realizing the destiny you were created to fulfill, you'll find more and more that the people around you are part of your team. Jack Canfield, the author of *Chicken Soup for the Soul,* says that each of us is a composite of the five people we spend the most time with in our lives. Certainly there's a lot of truth in that, so you should stop and think about those five people. Are you getting from them as much as you are giving? Are they challenging you or are they bringing you down?

Think of your life as a fantastic but sometimes perilous adventure in which you are allowed to take along just a few companions. As you move further along your priority pathway, more people will come into your life in partnership. You want to bring along people who will make that adventure a joyous and rewarding success. You want people who know how to read maps, people who can get under the hood and fix things that are broken, people who will appreciate the beauty and wonder of the trip you are on. You'll want to learn from other people who have already been where you want to go.

When you are growing and changing, you need to build a support system, a network of people who are sharing the work that you are doing and helping you stay steady, no matter how difficult things become. It's *hard* to make changes, and the last thing you want on your trip is people who complain, people who are constantly pointing out your mistakes and indecision, your fears and your faults. As Lou Holtz said, surround yourself with encouragers, with cheerleaders. Avoid people who suck out your energy and your self-confidence. Be alert to the subtle ways that people will try to make you give up all the hard gains you've achieved. You don't want to have to feel guilty about how your behavior is affecting someone else.

Do not go where you are tolerated. Go where you are celebrated.

As I said, it may be hard to realize that there are people in your life who are not helping you—people who are, in fact, making it more difficult for you to realize your dreams. I'm not saying that you should instantly shut anyone out of your life. But you may want to talk with such a person, to let that person know that you won't be held back from reaching your goals, and that you would like him or her to join you. Some will look only to their fears and sit back in their unhappiness. Others will rise to walk with you and grow with you.

There is a power in that kind of partnership, and you want to make it a reality. It provides a ready-made support group of family and friends who really care. You want to develop relationships that will strengthen you individually but also strengthen all of you as a group. I was watching the Discovery Channel with my children the other day and they were showing a nature film about wildebeest in Africa. A small bird called an oxpecker lives with the wildebeest in a perfect partnership. The wildebeest provides food and a home for the bird—it even lets the bird pull out its hair to make a nest. The oxpecker provides a cleaning service by eating the insects that attack the wildebeest. Plus if the bird spots a predator, it will run up and down the wildebeest's back, screeching until the big animal pays attention and heads for safety. And it's usually a partnership for life.

The Widening Ripples

As you bring about changes in yourself, it has the same effect as a rock thrown in a still pond: ever-widening circles. Your behavior may affect someone else.

We cannot help exchanging with the world, and it is our gain if that exchange is a gain for the world. And we can benefit the world when we have improved ourselves, even in small ways. I had a friend named Jim who worked in an office for a large corporation. He had quit smoking, but every time he went to a meeting the room was filled with smokers. And naturally, every once in a while someone would offer him a cigarette. He would decline with a comment such as "No thanks, I haven't had one of those in about five years. And I feel so much better that I don't think I'll ever smoke one again." Then he would go sit at the end of the table as far from the smokers as possible.

Eventually he noticed that one or two other people in the company would join him at the far end of the table, the breathing section. Over the next several months, the nonsmoking section kept growing and growing until finally the tables had turned and there were only a few people at the smokers' end. Eventually management decided to ban smoking in meetings altogether.

There will come a time when you want to share your good fortune, and returning the gift of life is the highest goal. Help yourself, but give others a full helping too. In fact, you may find that serving others well, offering them a good meal, is the most rewarding thing you can do. Life is not all about taking; it's also about giving back.

As you grow, you will begin to give to others; you will become the mentor, the helper, the teacher. Not only is that the natural consequence of the changes in yourself, it's also the next step up in the development cycle that you are cultivating in yourself. It's good for you too. The book of Proverbs says, "One man freely gives, yet grows all the richer; another withholds what he should give and only suffers want" (Proverbs 13:7).

> *Each one of us is setting an example for someone else, and each one of us has a responsibility to shape the future as we wish it to be.*
>
> —Gandhi

Perhaps we make a mistake thinking that the only way to improve ourselves is from the inside. The great psychologist Carl G. Jung expressed the idea in his book *Psychology and Religion* that the soul is for the most part outside the body. A contemporary philosopher, Thomas Moore, said of this idea, "If we were to think of the soul as being in the world, then maybe our work would be seen as a truly important aspect of our lives." Our soul is out there as much as it is in here, and in order to nurture it and care for it and grow it, we need to make the world a better place—a better place for it, a better place for ourselves, a better place for everyone.

- No life is full if it is isolated.
- Recognize which relationships are for reasons or seasons or a lifetime.
- What you make happen for someone else, life will make happen for you.

YOUR UTMOST LIVING JOURNAL

Think about all the people you connect to in your life. If you list them, you might be surprised at how many there have been—even people who are no longer in your life may still be affecting how you think and feel.

List the people you want to connect with more strongly.

_____

_____

_____

_____

_____

List the people you want to learn from. You might finish the thought: *I feel good when I've been around_____because . . .*

_____

_____

_____

_____

_____

_____

What about the people who teach you by offering a bad example? *I
don't feel good after I've been around_____because . . .*

_____

_____

_____

_____

_____

8

. . .

Avoiding Indigestion

Even when you eat carefully, there will be times when you come away with indigestion. You know what that feels like—that uncomfortable upset in your stomach that happens when your body just can't absorb something you've taken in. You don't like the feeling it gives you or the mood it puts you in. You just want to get rid of it. It's not bad enough for you to go to the doctor, so you go home and take some bicarbonate of soda, maybe drink a little ginger ale, and try to relax until it passes.

The same thing happens in life. No matter how well you prepare, there will be times when something happens that you didn't want and didn't intend. You make a mistake, your plan doesn't work, or something goes wrong that you didn't foresee. It can and will happen even though you've been working hard on all the things we've been talking about: you've focused on your goals, and you're starting to see some progress toward them. People in your life are perhaps beginning to look at you differently. Sometimes they ask you for your opinion, and they even listen to what you're saying. You're keeping track of your progress and making your goals clearer and more specific.

But then someone says something critical and other people agree. Or despite all your preparation about your diet, you lose control and go on a binge. Or no matter how hard you study and practice, you just aren't seeing any progress. That's indigestion. It can even make you feel like your whole plan is misguided. You just want to lie down and throw the whole problem, the whole project, the whole plan, right out the window.

A Setback Doesn't Have to Be a Step Back

One morning in the diner I see an old friend named Marvin looking morose. When I ask him what's the matter, I can barely hear him. "No, no, I'm fine," he says. "Just had some setbacks. I think maybe I have to rethink what I'm doing." When I ask him why, he doesn't really give me a clear answer.

You see this a lot. When people get down, it's like their voice gets down too—down to a whisper. Marvin had been on a roll with his new job in a computer game company, taking to it like a fish to water. When he started, he did everything he was asked to do, and he did it fast. He started early; he stayed late. He listened to everybody and he thought about what he heard.

"So then they asked me to evaluate one of the new game proposals. I was psyched. I spent three days and nights working on it. I had everything together—sales, reviews, industry expectations, stock prices—everything. I went to the meeting with all the suits. I even bought a suit." My look says surprise. "Well, I bought a sport jacket and a tie."

"And what happened?"

"And what happened? I'll tell you what happened. The Man—the guy who sits at the end of the table, can't be under fifty-five, whose fingers are too clunky to use even Wii, who's always chewing on a pencil, that guy says, 'It's garbage.' "

"That's all?"

"That's all. Moves on to the next project. I'm looking around the room and nobody's looking back at me. I might as well be dead."

"That's tough."

"I might as well be back at my old job. At least there nobody noticed me."

Winners got scars too.

—Johnny Cash

I can hardly hear him again, but I know what he's really saying: *It's too hard. Nobody cares. I don't need this kind of rejection after I worked so hard.* Even when you are on the path, when you know your goals, when you are letting your passion drive you, sometimes you are going to go off the road.

I worked once with a running back in the National Football League. He was at the top of his career when one season he began fumbling the ball. He'd get tackled and lose the ball. It became such a fear that he was afraid to carry the football, especially in crucial situations. I was able to help him, but the problem plagued him for the rest of his career. Even worse, he took the problem into his personal life. After he retired from the NFL, he received all kinds of offers of business opportunities that he could get involved in. But he decided not to take up any of them because he was afraid he would fumble it. His fear had become his vision of life. He was shrinking back from life, not rushing forward to grasp it. That's the way Marvin was feeling.

"So do you really want to go back to your old job?" I asked Marvin.

"Yes. No. I mean, I don't want to get dumped on like that again. What if I don't have the talent anyway? Why get beat up all the time? This isn't the first time I screwed up, you know. Even at the last job, they were always telling me what I did wrong."

The Hurt That Helps

We all have to face the fact of indigestion. There's always going to be an opposition to your mission. It might be big and it might be small. You're trying to lose weight and a new Krispy Kreme donut shop opens up across the street from you. You finally finish your degree and the rules change so that you need to take more credits to get the job you want. The opposition might be a direct result of your mission, as when I tried to join the Peace Corps only to discover that I had nothing to offer them. Or it might be completely unexpected and unrelated—just when you have made the time to start working on a new project that could change your life, your mother gets sick and you have to take care of her.

That's the way the cookie crumbles, people say, either with a laugh or with a sigh. There's a real truth in that. Life does give you some bad breaks and hard knocks. Cookies do crumble. That doesn't mean you shouldn't get back in the kitchen and start baking some new ones.

Setbacks simply are part of life. Nothing is ever going to go exactly the way you'd hoped or planned. Life is right, absolutely perfect, only about 10 percent of the time. One day in ten the sun will be shining, your mind will be clear, you have all the energy you need, you won't be arguing with anybody in your family, and your desk will be clean. One month a year you won't have to worry about money. One year every decade you'll be in perfect health and your car won't need major repairs.

> *The ultimate measure of a man*
> *is not where he stands in moments*
> *of comfort and convenience,*
> *but where he stands at times of*
> *challenge and controversy.*
>
> —Martin Luther King Jr.

What are you going to do with that other 90 percent of your life— those other nine days, those other eleven months, those other nine years? Are you going to wait until the good time comes again? Are you going to get a donut and a cup of coffee and sit in front of the television for the next decade?

No way. The important thing is to recognize that indigestion doesn't define your life. You're not going to sink into that bog; you're not going to shrink away from creating your utmost life. The reason you aren't going to do that is because you have that mission—your purpose—and you know to let your passions carry you forward. No matter what your abilities or knowledge now, God has equipped you with more potential than you can use in a lifetime. Get up and use it.

To think that you cannot be great does yourself a great injustice, and does God a great injustice as well. As the Bible says, if God takes care of the birds of the air, how much more will he take care of you? As beautiful, as necessary, as important as the birds are, they are not made in the image of God, as you are. Many times we try to do something with our own strength, and it may be too big for us. But it's just right for God.

You'll be able to use your supernatural strength—God's the super and you're the natural. God equips you to live up to your potential.

> *You have to accept whatever comes*
> *and the only important thing is that*
> *you meet it with courage and with*
> *the best you have to give.*
>
> —Eleanor Roosevelt

When something happens that makes you question your mission, have faith that it is only a step toward something much greater. As we said, make room for the big things in your life. Clear out the clutter of negative thoughts, self-doubt, and indecision. You have everything you need to drive past that roadblock, and I'm going to show you how to use it.

Once I was speaking at a large church in Los Angeles. Afterward a young man came up and said he wanted to do the same thing I did—he wanted to help people to improve their lives. Right then and there I decided I would give him my Bible. Of course, Bibles are very important to me, but that Bible was a special one. I had been speaking from that Bible for probably fifteen years. I knew every bend and curve of it and I had handwritten notes all through it. But I gave it to this young man and said, "You have a great future."

Several years later, this man tracked me down. He showed up on my doorstep and tried to return that Bible because he'd had some reverses. He said, "Tim, I've encountered a lot of obstacles and I've walked away from everything that I know is right and true. So I want to give this Bible back to you." I said, "It sounds to me like you need this Bible more than ever. I'm not going to take it back. This gift that I gave you will be a constant reminder of what I think about you. I think you're a world shaker and a history maker. I think you're somebody who will accomplish great things." Amazed, he smiled and said, "I can't believe you still believe in me." I told him that it was still early in the game of life and that I'd help him navigate through the challenges. He went on to do good things, and I know that you will too.

Think about how you felt the last time some person or some incident gave you indigestion in your life. What happened? First off, you lost your focus. You kept thinking about what went wrong. You cursed that thing. *It shouldn't have happened to me. It's not fair.* Well, you got that right. Life is not fair. Bad things shouldn't happen to good people. But that's the way it is. Ken Keyes said it: "No one that ever lived has ever had enough power, prestige, or knowledge to overcome the basic condition of all life—you win some and you lose some." After you cursed it, you might have nursed your misfortune for a while. Told your family about that terrible thing that just happened. Wailed to your friends about the injustice of it all.

Then maybe you rehearsed it for yourself and anyone who would listen. You went back over every step and imagined how it should have gone differently. Or you just sat back and pitied yourself. And what did you have once you had cursed, nursed, and rehearsed, as Zig Ziglar puts it? You still had indigestion.

Turn Your Mess into Your Message

Like Marvin, when something goes wrong, you may feel that you've failed. Generally, when we speak of failure, we're really saying that there is something inside us that wasn't adequate—a weakness, a blindness, a lack. We're ashamed that after all this work, we have nothing to show for it. That's not the way God sees it.

One of the most interesting and inspiring stories in the Bible is that of the prodigal son. I'm sure you all remember the story, but there may be a part of it that you missed. The prodigal son wanted to take his inheritance early, but when his father gave it to him, he went off and spent it all on riotous living. I think of that as lack-of-appreciation living. He didn't appreciate the gifts that he had, and he used them poorly. Eventually there came a time when he had nothing left; he squandered everything he had, the Bible says, and found himself in dire need.

When he came to his senses, he saw that he couldn't keep on living this way—even the people who worked for his father lived a better life than he was living. So he decided he'd go back home and at least try to get a regular job. He realized that he was going to be a failure unless he went back to the place that his gifts came from. He would always be an underachiever unless he returned to the source of his strength.

One of the things you can take away from this is that sometimes it's when we act badly that we see what we have to change about ourselves. It takes something going wrong, a bad example, to see which way is the right one.

When one door closes another door opens; but we so often look so long and so regretfully upon the closed door, that we do not see the ones which open for us.

—Alexander Graham Bell

His father, however, had an entirely different idea. His father saw his son with the eyes of compassion. Even when his son was in a bad way, his father was preparing for the son's restoration. While his son was living riotously, his father had the faith to make special sandals, a special robe, and a special ring for his son. The father planned for the party that would be held in his son's honor upon his return by preparing the fatted calf.

In the Bible the father says to his servants, "Get the fatted calf." Now, that doesn't mean that the servants went out into the field and wandered around until they saw the porkiest calf. In Greek, the father's words mean, "Get the appointed calf. Get the calf I marked for this day." He had to be thinking in advance. He knew his son would come back and come back strong, and he had already picked out a calf and was fattening it for the occasion. And a calf grows quickly, so the father knew it would be soon.

There are many good ideas for us here. First of all, you will come back from disappointments and delays; you will overcome the hindrances—it's certain. Second, when you do come back, when you return to the place in your head and your heart and your faith that your strength comes from, you will be rewarded. When something goes wrong, God is just pointing out where you need to learn something new, where you need to become stronger. And if you have the determination, you will become stronger.

> *Forget about the consequences of failure. Failure is only a temporary change in direction to set you straight for your next success.*
>
> —Denis Waitley

So there's no need to accuse yourself of a weakness or a deficiency after you hit a pothole in the road. Those negative thoughts are natural, but if you look at them carefully, you'll see that they aren't useful. Don't blame yourself—investigate the situation and see what you need to do better the next time. There's no point in blaming someone or something else—a colleague, a teammate, a spouse, the weather. What good does that do you? Other people aren't going to change. It doesn't help to bemoan your evil fate, because it's not going to change unless you make it change. The good thing you can do is to learn from what happened and change *yourself.*

When I was fifteen, I met a football player named Isaiah Robertson. Isaiah played for the Los Angeles Rams before they went to St. Louis. He was a linebacker, and six times was named All-Pro. He used to come around, and sometimes he'd show up at my baseball games driving a big Mercedes and looking great. More than ten years later, I was shocked to find out that Isaiah had become involved in drugs and lost much of what he'd gained over the years. He was in a desperate place.

I said to him, "I want you to do something radical. Come and live with me." And he did. I was then just finding some success speaking, and was even working with some professional sports teams. For the first few months, Isaiah was pretty much stuck in the past. We would walk and he would talk about chasing Roger Staubach or catching Robert Newhouse at the goal line—things I'd seen on *Monday Night Football.* But he always talked about his life in the past tense, as if it were a great life that was over.

It reminded me of a scripture in the Bible, Isaiah 43:18–19: "Forget about the former things and do not dwell on the past. For behold, God is doing a new thing." It's hard to embrace the new things when you're constantly looking back at the old thing. I told Isaiah, "Just because you failed, it doesn't mean your life is over. You don't have to stay where you are. In the midst of your challenges, you have to get up."

One day I was speaking at a meeting, and I saw a different Isaiah: his face was alive and shining. Afterward I asked him what had made the difference. He said, "Tim, I got it. I actually got it. Something big is about to happen in my life." He wasn't wrong. Things began to work for him, and he started a ranch for young boys who were having problems with drugs and alcohol. He called it the House of Isaiah. He had taken his test and turned it into his testimony, taken his mess and made it into his message. Today, hundreds of young people have come through the House of Isaiah and made an everlasting change in their lives—because one person decided to get back up.

The Reality of Change

Now that you've really embarked on the road to success, you'll be dealing with the realities of change—change in your life and change in yourself. Even though you won't be changing your whole life all at once, any kind of change can throw you off balance a little. It's not a comfortable feeling, and your first reaction might be to go back to the balance you had before. Even though it wasn't satisfying, at least you knew what it was. The better way to react is to find a new position of balance. Instead of the ease and comfort of sitting down, you can be in the active, forward-looking position of standing. Then walking. Then running.

> *Failure is the condiment that gives success its flavor.*
>
> —Truman Capote

Failure is life's attempt to teach you something. You can't succeed unless you fail. It's during that 90 percent of life that's not perfect that you are learning how to make it better. Henry Ford said, "Failure gives us the opportunity to begin again more intelligently." You can learn something when you get rejected, when you make a mistake, when you make a wrong turn. That's how you turn your mess into your message.

> *Flops are part of life's menu*
> *and I've never been a girl to*
> *miss out on any of the courses.*
>
> —Rosalind Russell

It's not the opposition to your mission that creates failure; it's how you react to it. Everyone creates their own reality based on their perception of the situation. Marvin just sat back and let the Pencil Chewer roll over him. That's natural enough. But what he can't do is to let it happen again. When you're faced with an opposition, you can grow or you can shrink; you can shout or you can whisper; you can stride or you can stumble. You have to make your acceptance, you have to make your correction, you have to make your success.

Focus on the Real Problem

The first step in getting over your setback is to regain your focus. Get out of that setback mentality. Tune back in to the Anything Is Possible Network and think about where you want to go and why you want to get there. Remember what you were aiming for and why. Look at what happened, accept it, and evaluate it. Don't pass sentence on yourself. Pass sentence on what happened. Figure out what you could have done better or how you could have avoided the problem.

Maybe you needed to learn something more about your goal or

about the company or the people around you. Maybe you needed to talk to someone else, to find a mentor who can help you. Ask him or her if your problem has ever happened to anyone else, and if so, how that person fixed it. Maybe it was just bad luck or bad timing. If so, vow that you will keep trying until you have good luck or until you make your luck good. You'll keep trying until the timing is good or until your timing is good.

Be honest with yourself, or ask others to be honest with you. Nobody gets it right the first time or even the second time. Let's take Marvin's video game. Maybe that kind of game was a total bust the last time the company tried it. Maybe if he had asked his colleagues, he might have learned that the Pencil Chewer hates games where you only have four options whenever there's a choice to be made. Maybe if he'd read more about what the competition was doing, he would have found out that another company was bringing out a very similar game a month earlier. Maybe the Pencil Chewer just slams everybody the first time they make a presentation. No, it's not fair. But it's life-learning.

Most success springs from an obstacle or failure. I became a cartoonist largely because I failed in my goal of becoming a successful executive.

—Scott Adams

The second arrow in your quiver is our old friend imagination. Take some time to get your feet back under you and feel the excitement of your dream. One thing that failure does is to teach you new ways to use your imagination. When you were setting goals for yourself, preparing yourself for success, you took the time to envision what it would be like when you succeeded. You imagined what it would look like, what it would feel like, what it would taste like. Now you have to do the same thing with opposition. Facing opposition, expecting opposition, and dealing with opposition are key steps to achieving success. You have to replace your setback mentality with a step-back mentality.

When you've experienced a setback, you have been given a new ingredient for your success. Once you change what went wrong, once you adjust either your behavior or your attitude, then you've firmed up the ground you stand on.

Life is constantly providing us
with new funds, new resources,
even when we are reduced to
immobility. In life's ledger there
is no such thing as frozen assets.

—Henry Miller

When things were going right, you didn't want to think about what it would feel like if they went left. You didn't want to get back to that place where things weren't going your way. But one of the things to learn on our path to success is never to avoid thinking about hard times, about failure, about making mistakes, about being alone. Psychologist Dr. Joyce Brothers says, "The person interested in success has to learn to view failure as a healthy, inevitable part of the process of getting to the top." An *inevitable* part. Readjust your vision of the future to include failure. Just don't let your subconscious hear that. Say to yourself, "Life will teach me lessons, sometimes in disguise. It's up to me to discover their real shape." It takes courage to face that fact, but once you do, you'll be better off.

Next, take another helping of persistence. Did you imagine that everything would go your way the first time? Were you reading the Cliff's Notes version of your life? Thomas Edison said that he tried more than a thousand different experiments before he made the light-bulb work. But he didn't describe them as a thousand failures—he said simply, "I took a thousand steps." If Edison had stopped after 999 experiments and just given up, he wouldn't have changed the world.

You will make mistakes as you're trying to accomplish your goal. You'll slip a Twinkie into your diet or sneak a cigarette. You'll make a proposal that is dismissed with a sneer. But as long as you learn from whatever happens, you've taken a step forward. You might have to learn 999 new things to reach your goal, the way Edison did, but each new idea, each new approach brought him one step closer to his goal. The important thing is not to stop. I couldn't get into the Peace Corps, but I didn't stop there. I investigated and navigated until I found the place I needed to be.

How to Succeed at Failing

So when you're going into a new situation, learning a new skill, you have to think and prepare. First you'll prepare for your success— research and study, think and practice, tone up your mental or physical muscles for whatever activity you'll be involved in. Then imagine what you will do if you don't succeed—if you don't wow the audience, if you don't get the highest score, if you don't get the job you've wanted. Think of it in terms of what you can learn. Decide then and there, before it happens, that you won't let it stop you. Have faith in your future. Don't expect perfection, but don't plan for collapse either.

Suppose you're trying to lose weight. You've planned your menus and calculated the nutritional values. You know when you're going to eat, what, and how much. Terrific. Now imagine that just as you're sitting down to dinner, you slip, bump into the cabinet, and break the vase that is your most treasured possession. It makes you want to pull out that container of Ben and Jerry's ice cream, grab the biggest spoon you can find, and devour the whole thing.

Now plan for that vase breaking. You'll definitely need—you definitely deserve—to reach back, relax, and regain your focus. Envision yourself having three spoonfuls of ice cream. Yes, you're going to give yourself something for that indigestion. But here's the most important part: You're going to enjoy that ice cream. You're not going to feel guilty about it, or feel that you've failed, or that you're weak. Having this ice cream is *part of the plan*—the plan for dealing with indigestion. Imagine that you'll sit there basking in the creamy sweetness of that delicious ice cream. When you're finished, you'll pull out your diet chart and plan what you will eat the next day, cut out a little here and there to make up the difference. Hey, it's just three spoonfuls, so it's not a big deal.

Make your plan, then work your plan.

—Norman Vincent Peale

Then you envision putting the ice cream away and cleaning up the mess. Imagine how much better you will feel because not only did you have the ice cream, you enjoyed it enough that you don't have to eat more. As I say, life is not a sprint, it's a marathon. You won't always succeed the first time, or the second, or the third—but that just means you will have more than one chance to succeed. In fact, you'll have many. Each time you fail, you'll have another clue about how to avoid failure the next time. The more you can learn to overcome the obstacles, to reposition that opposition to your mission, the more you will enjoy doing it.

Prepare and envision. See yourself overcoming the problems, see yourself answering your critics. The next time you're working on a presentation, imagine how to respond if your boss disparages your ideas. It could be as simple as being ready to ask your boss what was wrong—whether it was the way you presented your idea or the idea itself. You might find out that there was nothing wrong with the idea, but that you didn't get it across adequately. You've learned something.

If you add that you want to benefit from the boss's experience, you might gain an ally in the bargain. Even if your boss still doesn't accept your idea, you might get some help the next time.

Change and Challenge

Whenever we start to tune in to the Anything Is Possible Network, whenever we start to act on the purpose, passions, and priorities we've identified inside ourselves, we step into the river of change. In big ways or small, life is different.

Many people don't like change. They're happy to live within their comfort zone. They may even be afraid of change. They want to stay out of the storm. But to believe that you can avoid or evade change is a fantasy. The one thing constant in life is change, and you can either change with it or get left behind.

I hope that you are not reluctant to change and that you don't fear it. If you look back at your life, you'll see that you have changed over and over again. If you're not where you want to be in life, that doesn't mean that changing has failed you—in fact, it probably means that you haven't changed enough.

I hope that the three Ps—purpose, passions, and priorities—have given you a thirst for change, or at least a willingness to drink from that cup. But I also want you to realize that change will test you—more than that, it will proof you. *Proof* is a wonderful word. In addition to the usual meaning of evidence about something, it can also mean "to test for strength or durability." Change will do that to you. *Proof* also means "to treat or coat for the purpose of rendering resistant to damage or deterioration." Change will do that too—in resisting the opposition, you will build up your muscles.

When you face change head-on and when you examine and learn from your mistakes, when you fail forward, that's what happens to you. You become resistant to damage. You have been "proofed." Facing change will take that other essential nutrient, courage. There's a wonderful story in the Bible about the courage to change. In the gospel of Matthew (8:21–23), Jesus comes to the disciples by walking on the water during a great storm. The disciples can't see too well in the midst of the storm, so Peter calls out that if it's really Him, then He should tell Peter to walk across the waves to Him. So Jesus says, "Come," and Peter starts stepping over the waves. As long as he keeps his eyes on Jesus, Peter is able to walk on the water, but when he looks up to see what is happening with the storm and takes his eyes off Jesus, he sinks.

So Peter is able to overcome the obstacle and to take up the challenge as long as he keeps his eyes on the long-term goal. Storms will come, but as long as you keep your eyes on your purpose, keep the courage to focus just on your goal and nothing else, there is nothing you can't achieve.

We all face storms in life, and we have to learn to weather them. There are three ways. Some storms you walk through. You stay steadfast and remain patient in the face of the challenge. Some storms you calm, with the help of God's supernatural peace. And some storms you walk over. You do something you never thought you could do before. You take that job you didn't think you could do. You jump the facts, as I say. You ignore what everyone says and what's always been done before and you take up the challenge. You walk on water; you jump the facts.

When I was nineteen I couldn't get into the university I wanted, but by my early twenties I was teaching there.

If you want the rainbow, you have to put up with the rain.

Never let yesterday use up too much of today. If something bad happens one day, learn from it and move on, because you can be sure that something new will happen today. Life can be understood backward, but it must be lived forward.

- There is no such thing as failure—it's an opportunity to improve.
- Use imagination, focus, and persistence to come back from a setback.
- If you fall off your bicycle, get back on right away—don't let fear stop you.
- Look back at something that didn't work out as you'd planned. What went wrong and how can you change that outcome?

YOUR UTMOST LIVING JOURNAL

During the most difficult times of our lives, we are growing, changing, and learning even when we don't realize it. Think about such a time in your life. It may be difficult to think about, but it will be worth the effort. (And the more you do it, the easier it will become.) Start with something that happened many years ago.

How did you react? Did you lash out? Did you pull back within yourself for weeks or months? Did you reach out to others for help?

How long did it take until you felt comfortable again?

What helped you the most to get your balance back?

How did you change after it?

_____

_____

_____

_____

_____

Looking back years later, does it seem like a turning point in your life? What new strengths did you gain from it?

_____

_____

_____

_____

_____

_____

_____

9

. . .

Turning the Desert
into Dessert

Selene comes into the diner, and she looks torn up from the floor up. She cries, "My company is downsizing. They laid me off." Suddenly everything she had accomplished, all the progress she had made, had vanished, along with her salary and her health insurance. That's not just a setback. That's a disaster. That's when you ask with real anguish, *Why me? Why did this have to happen to me? I didn't do anything wrong! I did everything I could!*

"I give up!" Selene yells, "I don't care about designing! I just want a safe job that will always be there. I want someone to take care of me!"

In the last chapter, we talked about how to overcome setbacks and obstacles with motivation and focus and how to use your mistakes to regain your forward momentum. In this chapter I'd like to talk more about the uses of adversity—those really powerful moments of life that knock you off your feet emotionally. No matter how devastating they are when they happen, they are still a part of the plan that God has designed for you.

Nothing that you experience in life is worthless; no struggle is pointless, no loss is without its subsequent reward. I tell Selene that she's survived bad times before, and ask if she'll be receiving unemployment insurance. "I will. And I have a little saved up. And they're letting me stay a month to clean things up. Find a job, really."

"And they usually extend the health benefits at least for a while."

"Yeah. Three months or something like that. Then I have to pay for it."

"You think you should get sick right away, then?"

She throws a sugar packet at me, and actually can't hide a smile for a second.

"You learned a lot at that company, didn't you?"

She says she did, and we talk a bit about jobs. I ask her about the downsizing. "Yeah, they were bought by one of those conglomerates that figured that it could fire half the combined staff as long as the ones who were left worked twice as hard."

"You had some compliments from some of the clients, didn't you?"

"Well, a couple."

"Think they'd hire you freelance?"

I'm just trying to get Selene to count her blessings. One of the things I learned was that whenever you're faced with a true setback, one of those out-of-the-blue storms that turns your life upside down, the first thing you need is gratitude.

That may seem strange, even impossible, but turning away from your negatives to look at your positives is a powerful tool. Pull yourself together and be grateful for what you have. It may be your faith, it may be your family, it may be your education, it may be your experience. Look to see what you've got and you may be surprised at how much there is. If you've been working on your plan and developing your skills, you have more than before. And there will be much more to come. There are times when real life hits you with such force that you're reeling, almost incapable of dealing with the pain of the situation. Those are the times you need gratitude and the times it will do the most for you. Gratitude is one of the most energizing and powerful emotions you can ever develop.

One of my favorite stories is of Saul, who became the Apostle Paul. Now Saul, before he became a disciple, was famous for persecuting Christians. He had people thrown into bags of snakes, had people's arms cut off, had people burned. But God knew that he was a strong and loyal person who would be just as strong and loyal in the service of Christ, if only he could understand. Jesus came to him in a blinding light and asked him, "Why are you persecuting my people?" Saul became a Christian and wanted to become one of the disciples.

But the disciples rejected him. It's not hard to imagine why. So he went into the desert and spent years there before he came back to preach. In Philippi, he and his companion Silas were beaten and whipped. Then they put him in jail, in the stocks.

> *It is in suffering that we are*
> *withdrawn from the bright*
> *superficial film of existence,*
> *from the sway of time and*
> *mere things, and find ourselves in*
> *the presence of a profounder truth.*
>
> —Yves M. Congar

Saul was hardly in a comfortable position, but the Bible says that he began to sing the praises of the Lord. He knew that the Lord had a plan for him, and in the midst of his suffering, he was grateful. For Paul, it was important to feel that gratitude, and the feeling was so strong he simply began to sing. Around midnight, an earthquake destroyed the jail and set Paul and Silas free.

When you are on the left, that earthquake will come inside you. The thing about gratitude is that it can set you right, can set you onto that right kind of feeling even when you are as far left as you can go. Gratitude is not just a wish and a hope. Gratitude is a recognition and an assertion that there is a plan, that there is a reason, that there is a promise, and that you can take advantage of them.

One of the most amazing examples of gratitude that I know is the story of Aimee Mullins. Aimee is a tremendous success as an athlete and a fashion model. Aimee is also a double amputee.

She was born with a bone missing from both of her legs, and her parents made the heartbreaking but courageous decision to have both her legs amputated when she was one year old so that she would be able to walk with prosthetic limbs. She literally took her disability in stride and could walk by the age of two.

Aimee says, "I decided at an early age to transform any setbacks into strengths and tackle them head-on." She did everything her brothers did—she swam, played soccer, skied, and had her own paper route. In college she competed with able-bodied athletes.

Then she decided to become a fashion model. "As a model, I can confront society's emphasis on physical perfection. There is no ideal body. Mine is imperfect, and I can't change that—but I can still be attractive. Confidence is the sexiest thing a woman can have! The truth is, I'm sort of lucky to have this body, because it forced me to find my strength and beauty within."

Gratitude for what you have can take you far, maybe even start to bring you out of the desert. It also takes courage: the courage to say that the past is in the past, the courage to look realistically at where you are.

I remember once being in Hawaii. Now, you know that people surf in Hawaii because the waves are big there. They are big and they don't ever stop. So there I was in these big waves and I wasn't used to them. A wave would come and knock me down. I'd try to get up and then another wave would come and knock me down again. I'd get up, and *bam*—another wave would knock me down. And another and another and another, until finally one of them pulled my swimsuit right off me. I was tired, I was hurting, I was naked, and here comes another wave. I couldn't even get out of the ocean until I found my swimsuit.

It makes me laugh now, but isn't that the way life is? You think you're ready to take a step out of the swamp you're in, and then something hits you and knocks you back down.

A Season on the Left

That kind of situation is what I call being on the left. *Left,* according to the dictionary, means "to abandon or forsake, to remove oneself from participating in." Everybody wants to be right, to get it right. It's a natural desire, but not always the best thing for you. The fact is, you're going to spend some time on the other side, on the left. It can be painful, it can be lonely, it can be devastating.

Tim Allen knows what it feels like, and I can relate. When he was eleven years old, his father was killed by a drunk driver. Everything changed for him. As he describes it, "One day, a part of your emotional connective tissue is there, the next it's not—and you have this black gaping hole. If you don't rake it over and plant something else, it eventually fills up with a kind of mud." That's a good description of being on the left—and how bad it can be. "I didn't have any idea what to do with the fact that the world is a very cruel place."

Maybe it's not an accident that Tim Allen also studied philosophy when he went to college and comparative religion after that. But he also began drinking and doing drugs, trying to medicate the pain that was in his soul. It got so bad that he wound up in jail and in AA. That was where he began to turn a corner. "There was a moment when I felt a direct connection with that which brought me here. Through feeling that connection—that there's a purpose to this whole thing—I can say, 'It's going to be all right.' "

It's funny, isn't it? Two Tims who were hit with the same punch but went very different ways with it—and then came back to a similar place. Because it is going to be all right, with that connection to the Spirit that moves us all.

Tim Allen spent a long season on the left, but he also became a hugely successful and highly admired actor and comedian. Is there a connection there? I believe there is. Some of you are probably thinking that you're glad you haven't been thrown to the left. *Whew,* you're thinking, *I've had some bad times, but nothing ever like that! I don't need that kind of grief!* But you're looking at it with your eyes, from your point of view. I think if you look at it with a God's-eye point of view, it might look a little different.

---

*No pain, no palm; no thorns,
no throne; no gall, no glory;
no cross, no crown.*

—William Penn

I want to tell you a story, a story from the Bible, but I hope you'll see that it's not a story that speaks only to believers. It tells a truth that is as true for me as it is for you and for the person on the bus next to you. It's just a story that tells a truth about the left.

It's the story of Moses, and I would bet that all of you have heard it once, but maybe only in the short version. Let me try to give it some context and background. Moses had been found in the reeds as a baby and was taken to Pharaoh's daughter, who adopted him. So even though he was orphaned, that wasn't the cause of his time on the left. In fact, just the opposite. He was brought up with love and care. He was given the best education, groomed to be one of Egypt's aristocrats.

Then one day, he went to see his people, the Hebrews, as they were working in the fields. There he saw an Egyptian beating a Hebrew, and when Moses realized that there was no one around watching, he killed the Egyptian. The next day he went out again to the fields and saw two Hebrews fighting, and he asked them why. Now, remember that Moses was one of the rulers—though he had been born Jewish—and the two Hebrews he confronted saw him only as an overlord. They were frightened.

"Who made you ruler and judge over us?" one of the men asked. "Are you thinking of killing me as you killed the Egyptian?"

Moses became afraid. *Somebody saw me kill that Egyptian,* he thought. *I've got to get out of here.* He was right too. All of a sudden, his life was turned upside down. He had made one bad decision, and now he was on the left instead of the right. Pharaoh tried to have him killed, but Moses escaped to a place in the desert called Midian. There he helped some women at a watering hole, and they took him in. Their father naturally wanted his daughters to marry, and Moses looked as good as anyone else who had come along. So Moses married the eldest daughter, Zipporah, and stayed to work for her father in the desert.

So there Moses was in the desert. He was in a bad way. He was thinking, *What happened to all that ease and comfort that was my life?* He was taking care of sheep. All his old friends had rejected him. He was wandering in the desert and asking what his faith could do for him. That means he was wondering what happened to his God idea. In

Egypt, he had thought he had one, but he was wrong. It disappeared and he was left without purpose. He felt, says the Bible, like an alien in a foreign land.

> *Call the world if you please "the vale*
> *of soul-making." Then you will find*
> *out the use of the world.*
>
> —John Keats

Everyone—you, me, Moses, Pharaoh—has moments when everything seems bleak. Moments when we feel forsaken, when we're no longer sure that the path that seemed to shine so brightly is the one we are able to follow. We are in the desert.

So what is the point of being in the desert?

"Tim," you say, "what are you talking about? There's no point in being in the desert. The desert is left and it's the place everyone wants to leave. There is nothing *there*—that's why they call it the desert."

> *Whatsoever things are true,*
> *whatsoever things are noble,*
> *whatsoever things are pure, think on*
> *these things.*
>
> —Philippians 4:8

I've been in the desert and I can tell you that there is much to learn there. I'd decided to go to a seminary so that I could learn biblical principles, a truly Christian vision of life that would allow me to help others. I started studying harder, trying to do better in school. I investigated, tried one university, but it turned me down. You can see that I'm not getting any special favors here. The Peace Corps, the university—they're telling me something.

But finally I navigated my way to a small school in Lakeland, Florida. Yep, from Los Angeles, California, to Lakeland, Florida. I tell you, when I got there, I knew what it felt like to be an alien in a foreign land. God took me from dancing at Dillon's downtown, called me to be a minister, and landed me in a Bible college with a bunch of people I did not get. We didn't come together—on music, on reading (except the Bible), on what to do on a Friday night. I could not relate to anybody. I was a devout person, but compared to the other students, I had barely put my toe in the water.

I had nothing to do. I'd get in my Honda Civic and drive around Lakeland and wonder what to do. What I did do was get lonely. I got so lonely my bones would ache. Not only could I not get a date, I couldn't find anybody on that campus I wanted to date. I'd dress up on a Friday night just to see how good I'd look if I *did* go out. I couldn't help thinking, *God, this is not* right. *I went from all the energy of my friends in Hollywood, the energy of the nightclubs, and here I am where there's a* blackout. *I'm an* alien.

At some point I realized I had to make the most of my left experience. I didn't know what else to do, so I studied the Bible. I started memorizing scripture. I was totally misunderstood and rejected, and all I had was Him. I had nothing else to do, so I prayed. I had nothing else to do, so I studied, went to meetings, watched people, listened to the ministers. I had nothing else to do but to go deep and get stronger, and that's what I did. Your time on the left can be a desert, or you can make it into dessert. Your life is what you make of it. Look around, and most of all look inside you. I did, and I reached the point where I actually enjoyed my own company. I studied the Bible and I got comfortable with myself.

I might not ever have done that if I had not had that time on the left. What would have happened if I had decided to leave school and head back to Hollywood? I would have slipped back into my old ways, and probably given up on my dreams of helping people. I'm glad I didn't; I'm glad I spent those years in the desert.

Most of us think that we've got to get out of the desert. We've been taught that left is wrong, and we've got to get back right. But those left experiences are what bring you the character, wisdom, and strength that make all things possible. I believe that there is a season of left that you should not try to escape because that's the time when you go deeper and deeper into yourself. You test yourself, you face down your fears, and you get stronger and stronger. Left will give you strength to stay right when the right finally comes. It's the painful experiences of left that help you to stay right in the right times.

Character cannot be developed in ease and quiet. Only through experience of trial and suffering can the soul be strengthened, vision cleared, ambition inspired, and success achieved.

—Helen Keller

Left will bring you the wisdom that you need. It makes you tougher. You can handle pain. You can handle pressure. You can handle rejection. You don't bow, you don't bend, you don't cower. The doctors call it post-traumatic growth, which is what happens when you face a challenge and come to grips with it. That test tears something down in you and builds something up, which is exactly what happens when you build up your body's strength. When you're exercising really hard, you actually tear muscles down and they are replaced by stronger muscles.

The Bible says in James 1:2, "Count it all joy when you go through trials." The testing develops inward strength and perseverance. You don't get handed out inner strength at Wal-Mart. And you don't build it up in a day. Some people have the will for it, but they don't have the strength because they haven't been on the left long enough.

> *Mishaps are like knives, that either serve us or cut us, as we grasp them by the blade or the handle.*
>
> —James Russell Lowell

Sometimes the best lessons are the ones that are learned slowly, so slowly that you can learn them deep inside you, so deep inside you that they come out of your pores. The bigger the right, the bigger the destiny, the longer you may spend on the left. God is taking time with you. It takes time to make a masterpiece.

Moses didn't see the whole picture. God saw that Moses would lead thousands of people through the desert, but the boy found in the bulrushes wasn't going to be able to do that on his charisma. Moses wasn't going to change the world because of his days among Egypt's pampered elite. He had to have depth, he had to have strength. When they were in the desert, the Israelites complained. They complained that there wasn't enough food, that there wasn't enough water. They complained that Moses had disrupted their lives without giving them anything in return. But Moses had been torn down and built up again. He had been on the left long enough that he could carry all of them on his back to the Promised Land.

The Life That's Left Is Abundant

Of course it's painful and wearying to be left. If you are there now, I cannot give you a magic formula that will change your life tomorrow. What I can do is tell you that your time there need not be wasted. You can turn your desert into a sanctuary—spend some time thinking about what you're doing on this planet. Spend some time investigating. You can turn your desert into a library; you can take time to study and learn. Read Shakespeare, read the Bible. Read about the people who have accomplished great things. You'll find that very often they went through their own desert years. Look for the good parts of the life you have rather than rehearsing the bad parts. Be grateful for what you have and what you can gain. And don't try to get away just for the sake of escaping.

Your Questions Will Give You the Answers

But how do you get through that time on the left? Well, there's a special kind of strength that the left can grow in you, and it can only be grown on the left, in the desert. The right can never teach it to you.

You never know how long you're going to be left rather than right. You will not come out of the left until you've learned what you need to know in order to succeed on the right. If you do, you may well find yourself back on the left because it's not as if the right is a picnic. There is a season to all things, and it is a season during which you are preparing yourself. It's just like when you're marinating a steak—the longer you do it, the stronger and fuller the taste will be once you take it out.

Ask yourself those questions you asked in despair, but ask them in good faith and with a humble heart. Where are you exactly? You're off your track, you're out of your groove, but where has that put you? Remember all that planning you've done and remember that you are not where you were. You're feeling the heat, but you remember the cool.

How did you get where you are? What actually happened before you hit the desert? Was there something from outside that tore into your life? An illness, an accident, an unexpected loss? It can't be any worse than what happened to a friend of mine. His leg had to be amputated. But when I walked into his hospital room, he was singing. "Thank God they didn't take off the other leg," he said. Things might be bad, but they could be worse. Like me when those waves knocked me over, you will get up again and make use of what you have to get back in shape.

You may have to readjust your goals—probably you will have some new ones that you will have to accomplish before you start again on the ones you had before. But don't give up on them. Anything is possible. Use your imagination to visualize where you want to be; use your head to plan how to reach that; use your faith to keep you focused.

What are you doing here? You may be in the desert, but what exactly are you doing? You may find some surprising answers. What can you do? Is there no way to find shade? What is it that you can be grateful for? What is it that you have learned about yourself that put you here?

Focus on the actual things that you are doing—your actions, your habits, your thoughts. If you are thinking only negative thoughts, then you need to sweep them away. I'm not saying that you can make your troubles go away, but with faith and gratitude you can take your focus off your troubles. Broom that gloom, and make room for the blossoms in your heart to bloom. Say aloud and loud what you are striving for, and say it in a positive way.

How long are you going to be in the desert before things start to get better? You're going to be there as long as you need to be. Your time on the left is a time for seasoning, for marinating. You are absorbing the thoughts and the talents that you need to get back on the road to your utmost life. You are already becoming a different person, a stronger person. It's happening.

Yesterday is a canceled check;
tomorrow is a promissory note. Today
is the only cash you have.
Spend it wisely.

—Kay Lyons

Being in the desert is a learning time. It can be a healing time. It can be a time when you get comfortable again with following your God idea because you study it. Or you may find that it was not what you thought it was. You may realize that there's a different way to fulfill your purpose.

We must use time as a tool,
not as a couch.

—John F. Kennedy

There was once a man who had a stroke that left him unable to talk. He'd been an actor all his life, a very successful actor. How could he be an actor if he couldn't talk? He needed to learn to speak all over again—where to put his tongue, how to use the muscles of his mouth, his throat, his lips. Things that he had always taken for granted suddenly became gigantic efforts.

He thought of suicide. He found a gun and put two bullets in it. After briefly hesitating over whether he should put it to his temple or his mouth, he chose the latter.

He hit himself in the tooth. "Ow!" He pulled the gun out and started to laugh hysterically. His own clumsiness had kept him from suicide. Finally he began to think about how selfish an act suicide was, how many people would be left behind to mourn and clean up the mess. He is Kirk Douglas, and he wrote a book about his experience. Ten years later, he's still doing exercises and writing books. So when you're feeling down, and feeling down on yourself, remember Kirk's tooth.

Three Steps and Out

There are three steps you can take in the desert that will help you find your way out when you're ready: Step back, step out, and step up.

Kirk's tooth made him step outside of the immediate situation and take a look at it without self-pity or remorse. He took a step back. There's nothing like a little humor to do that, but I know it's hard sometimes to find any humor in being in the desert. It's been famously said that laughter is the best medicine, and although it's still not clear whether a good sense of humor means you live longer, a good laugh not only picks up your spirits, it helps you to put a little distance between you and your problems. Go see a comedy, visit that friend who always makes you laugh, play with some children.

But however you do it, you need to take a walk around your situation. Try to get some distance on it and—here's the hard part—take your own fears and worries and self-criticism out of it. Imagine, for instance, describing it to the Apostle Paul, when he was in prison in Philippi.

Now let me remind you what kind of day Paul had been having.

He'd been beaten and he'd been whipped thirty-nine times, all for try-ing to preach the gospel. After the beatings, his Roman jailers put him in the stocks. Sometimes the holes in the stocks were set so far apart that they would break the pelvic bones of the victim. That was kind of a bonus for the Romans.

> *Trust thyself: every heart vibrates to*
> *that iron string.*
>
> —Ralph Waldo Emerson

So there was Paul, bleeding, with his legs pulled way apart. Suppose you were to go up to him and say, "Hey, Paul, you got a minute? I have some things that have been bothering me and I thought you might help." Paul would be humming a little tune in praise of the Lord, but he might look up and say something like, "Go right ahead. Have a seat. I'd make room for you, but these stocks are pretty heavy."

So you sit down and you tell him all about your divorce and how much debt your rat-fink ex left you with and how hard it is to keep working at the same dull job every day. Now the reason you've decided to tell this to Paul is that you can be pretty sure he's not going to look at you and say, "Hey, you think you've got problems?" No, in fact, Paul is probably going to be sympathetic and start asking you about your life and about ways you might be able to make it better. And then once you've thought of a few things and started to wonder how you're going to do them, he will say, "Trust in the Lord." That's just before that earthquake. So you see what trust can do.

Trust in the Lord that He is preparing you for something greater. Trust in yourself—trust that all the things you're going through are ways for you to build your strength. Accept that this time, this time that seems so hard, is the time you need in order to take advantage of the good times. Because even if times are good, they are likely not going to be easy.

Faith is the substance of things hoped for, the evidence of things not seen.

—Hebrews 11:1

That trust will let you step back from your problems. Yes, it's a bad time, but it could be worse. Yes, it's hard now, but it will become easier. Yes, there seems to be no way out, but whenever a door closes, another door opens. Even Paul doubted his strength and asked the Lord for help. The Lord said, "My strength is made perfect through weakness." Trust. Be cool. Be content. Paul says, "I am content when I am down and I am content when I am up."

One of the things I learned during those lonely days at college was to look at the big picture and to accept it. Remember that everything that happens to you is meant to happen to you. You have to go through it in order to get to it. Sometimes you have to go through hell in order to get to heaven because going through is what makes you strong enough and dedicated enough to keep on. But you'll get there faster when you are energized by trust and gratitude. I want a skip in my step and a glide in my stride even when I'm left. We must learn to enjoy the trip, not worry about when we're going to get there.

I learned to be content at that school. I learned I could be content when I was on the right and I could be content when I was on the left. I could go through hell and still be content. That's how to have a good day every day. Contentment is not passivity; it doesn't mean that you're letting people walk all over you. Contentment is a harboring of your strength. It means not fighting battles when you don't have a real opposition or a way to fight them. How long do you fret over the person who honked at you this morning because you didn't turn fast enough? How many snappy comebacks did you think of—hours later—to answer that co-worker's dig at you?

Contentment means keeping your focus on the things that are important to you and to God, not to other people. Richard Carlson said, "Don't sweat the small stuff . . . and it's all small stuff." When you don't sweat the things that are distracting you from your real purpose, your God idea, you have strength to go out and do the things you need to do. You have strength to work and grow and learn because you are not wasting your energy wailing and moaning. You are singing.

> *I'm always making a comeback but
> nobody ever tells me where I've been.*
>
> —Billie Holiday

If things are not the way you want them (they usually aren't), step back. If you don't know what to do next, step back. Step back so that you can get some distance from where you are and see it from a God's-eye view. Come to terms with your situation. Accept the fact that it won't be a steady upward climb to perfection; it may be a roller-coaster ride or it may be a series of plateaus. But no matter what, you will keep your eyes on the prize. From the space shuttle *Discovery,* even the tallest mountains on earth seem like small irregularities in the beautiful curve of the planet. When you get out of the desert, you will see that it was a hot summer day during a year of weather of all kinds. When you get back from the left, you will see that it was just a bend in the ongoing curve of your life.

When you know that you're in the desert but are content to seek and reap the harvest it offers, you can take the second step—step out. Even when you're feeling bad, when you're having that spiritual bad hair day, you have to be open to experience. God has prepared your comeback for you; don't miss it. He needs your cooperation. If you live in fear of life, if you are not willing to go out even when you have a bad hair day, you may miss the one experience that will show you how capable you can be. You may miss meeting a person who can offer you the help you need. You may not find the knowledge that will open your mind and your heart to the greater good that awaits you.

> *Don't give God instructions; just
> report for duty.*
>
> —Corrie ten Boom

But in order to do that, you have to have those experiences, you need the preparation, you need the relationships. You cannot do anything unless you've done something—as the old proverb says, a journey of a thousand miles starts with a single step. Don't feel that you need to change the world, and don't disdain the small things. Don't try to run a marathon in a day; start by walking around the block. Go see your mother and spend some time with her; cook dinner for her. Go bowling and don't worry about the score. The important thing is to sweep out the thoughts that prevent you from acting, doing, living. Do not disdain making yourself feel better. Do not disdain your friends when they offer help.

When I was in seminary in California we used to go down to Hollywood and talk to young people who were runaways and try to talk them into homes that would help them make their lives better. One night a group of us saw a girl on Sunset Boulevard. Men were driving by and yelling horrible things at her. I and two people with me watched this sadly, and decided to approach her to see if we could help. Sometimes people just told us to go away, which we would, but this girl didn't.

Her name was Katrina. She was from the Midwest, but she now found herself walking the streets of Hollywood to earn money. She was nineteen and she already had a child. She was jaded by life and angry, especially at men, for things that had happened to her. After we'd talked a bit, I asked her, "When you were a little girl riding your bicycle, did you ever think you'd be standing on a street corner on Sunset Boulevard with men yelling rude things at you?"

She immediately began to cry, and finally whispered, "Not at all." We ended up finding her a very special place that helped runaway girls. They were known for helping people find their true self. For a month I didn't see her, because she had to go through detox, but when my team was finally able to see her, she was a completely different person. Her face was alive, her posture was straight and strong. I said, "Oh my goodness! What did they do to you?" She smiled and said, "They washed my brain. You know that scripture in the Bible, Philippians 4:8?" she asked, and then quoted it: " 'Whatsover things are pure, whatsoever things are true, whatsoever things are good, think on these things.' Tim, I've decided to forget about my past and look forward to my future." She never looked back; she only got better and stronger. Her life had looked so terrible, but she listened to people who wanted to help her. She decided that if she was going to fail, she was going to fail forward, into the mercy of God.

Get Ahead on the Way Ahead

The third step is to step out. Step out of the desert. Get back on that bicycle and try to ride it again, knowing that if you fall, you will be able to get back on it. When you can be content with the good and with the bad, you will have the confidence you need to say yes to your purpose. You'll be able to tune in to the Anything Is Possible Network again, to go back to your goals and passions and priorities and take up the challenge again. You won't try to fly on the false security that you will never fall short again; you will be able to think of failures and faults and be prepared to learn from them, to squeeze the meaning out of them and make them show you how to do things better.

It may take a week, it may take a month, it may take a year. As I said, it will happen when God has determined it will happen, but you have to be ready to allow it to happen to you. When you are content with your life as it is, you will have the strength to make your life as it should be. You've accepted where you are, and looked for ways to make it better, to make yourself better.

- When disaster strikes, meet it with acceptance and gratitude— accept its reality and be grateful for what you have.
- Adversity can strengthen you; don't give up, but don't give in.
- Take your time, recall your purpose, regain your focus, reignite your passions.

YOUR UTMOST LIVING JOURNAL

Make your vision of the future rock solid by imagining the worst that can happen to you when you are living your utmost life.

How will it affect your daily life and your free time?

_____

_____

_____

_____

_____

How do you want your family and friends to react? Let them know what you hope for, both from yourself and from them.

_____

_____

_____

_____

_____

If someone taunts you or tempts you or criticizes you, what will you say?

_____

_____

Imagine that you've accomplished your goal. What will you do next?

1 0

. . .

Utmost Living
Is a Cuisine,
Not Just a Recipe

The dictionary defines *cuisine* as "a style or quality of cooking." That is, it's the way you do things, not just a collection of recipes or even a collection of techniques. There's also an older meaning of *cuisine*, a meaning that it still has in French, Italian, and other European languages. That is "kitchen," the place where you make delicious things. Your life is not a workshop, a place where you carry out the same tasks and fulfill the same duties every day. It is a laboratory and a studio—a place where you are constantly experimenting and creating, a place that combines science and art. It's a kitchen and style of living.

I've given you a wide array of tools and techniques and ingredients that you can use to create an utmost life, but I also want you to think of your life as a cuisine, as a way of doing things. As the ancient proverb says, "Give a man a fish and he will eat tonight; teach him how to fish and he will eat for a lifetime."

Let's review some of the techniques you've learned:

1. The 3 Ps—the fundamentals that help you understand yourself and make plans by making clear your purpose, your passions, and your priorities.

2. Imagination, which can literally change your life by raising the roof on your dreams. Any dream that you can envision completely and vividly can come true—and it will come true if you believe in yourself and the gifts that you have been given. Imagination provides the spark and the energy that creates motivation.

3. Of course you can't just lie on the couch and imagine that life. You reach your goals with focus and courage.

4. When you hit a bad time and find yourself in the desert, you step back, step out, and step up from the desert into a renewed and reinvigorated energy to carry you forward.

All of these tactics and strategies will help you in dealing with specific problems in your life—habits you want to change, aspects of your life you want to improve—and if you apply them consistently and persistently, I am confident that you will succeed at overcoming any specific problem. But what happens when you succeed? What lies on the other side of success? There are actually two possible outcomes, and the one I want to deal with first is that, ironically, success can trip you up.

Plan for the Consequences of Success

Now is the time to start looking at who you will be and what you will do when you reach your goal. The fundamental thing you must accept and plan for is that you will be a different person when you get there, and that difference will ripple across your life in big or small waves. But big or small, they can sink you when you least expect it. In fact, you need to start preparing yourself to be that different person. The story of my friend Cathy is a perfect example.

Cathy was very overweight. For her health alone, she really needed to lose a hundred pounds. She had been overweight her whole life, had reached her thirties without ever having a date, though she was a cheerful and enjoyable companion. On Fridays she sat home alone, went to a movie by herself, or maybe babysat for some friends. Not only that, she had come to feel comfortable about her weight and the restrictions it put on her life. On the whole, she was satisfied with her life and where it was going. She was past that divine dissatisfaction that can set you on the path to a better life.

Then one day she heard about a new diet that was medically supervised, and she had an insight that this might be the kind of thing she needed. She signed up for the program and followed carefully all the directions the staff gave her. What she was to eat, how to exercise—everything was predetermined and taken care of for her. And lo and behold, she was a success. She lost the weight and looked terrific. A friend set her up on a blind date and it went so well that her date asked her out again. Seems like just what Cathy wanted, right?

Not exactly. Too often, we think that if we hit a weight that doctors recommend, everything else in our lives will be great, but of course it usually doesn't work out that way. Not quite. Because the medical supervision had taken all the responsibility off her, Cathy hadn't actually prepared herself. She wasn't mentally ready to change this much. She was terrified of the new responsibility of being thin; she couldn't just blame her problems on her weight. If this new person in her life didn't continue to call her for dates, he couldn't be reacting to her weight. That was not an excuse any longer. If she wasn't given top assignments at work, it wasn't because of a prejudice about excess poundage. If she was home alone, it wasn't because she couldn't be thin like the people in the ads. She had nowhere to hide.

We've already discussed envisioning your utmost life in all its positive aspects, and we've even talked about preparing for failures and bouncing back from them. But as you're transforming your life, you need to prepare yourself for the difficulties that can be part of your success, the differences that will become part of your life and how the people around you will be different toward you. You will look ahead so that when an opposition to your mission arises, you are ready to reposition yourself to overcome it.

> *It is better to look ahead and prepare*
> *than to look back and regret.*
>
> —Jackie Joyner-Kersee

Cathy hadn't spent enough time in the contemplation stage of change—which wasn't really her fault, since the diet was supposed to do everything for her. She wasn't subconsciously ready to be thin, and before long she had gained back all the weight she'd lost. She was right back where she started. Cathy isn't alone, or even unusual, in that predicament. Most people who succeed in dieting and reach the weight they have been aiming at regain the weight they lost, slowly or quickly. One reason for that is purely physical—our bodies find a certain weight range to be the most comfortable. But even people who have lost weight within their comfort range have trouble keeping the pounds off. There are two reasons for that.

One is that they haven't actually changed. They have succeeded in denying themselves the things they used to crave—*but they still crave them.* That's a recipe for disaster, and I hope what you've learned so far has made it clear that to change successfully, you will crave different things—exercise instead of ice cream, for instance.

The second reason people may regain weight is that they don't know what to do next. They don't want to lose more weight (either because it's unhealthy or because it's unnecessary) and there's nothing deeply satisfying about stepping on a scale and seeing that, yep, you weigh the same as you did last week. *Losing* weight has been the emotional center of their lives, and once they're at their ideal weight, they have lost that center.

So make planning for success a part of your plan. Think about your 3 Ps—purpose, passions, and priorities—get time on your side, and find the right people for the rest of your life.

1. During those hours when you are gritting your teeth to avoid eating the plate of cookies your mother baked for you, think about what you could do with all that extra emotional energy. What is the next step in fulfilling your purpose in life? Or is there one of your passions that will replace the goal of losing weight?
2. Suppose you're spending five days a week at the health club. Is that what you want to be doing when you've reached your goal? If so, no problem, but if you envision reducing your exercise time, work that into your plan.
3. Is your support network for losing weight going to be a help in getting beyond losing weight? Are they people who are focused on only one thing, or will they be people who can accompany you *past* the goal line?

The things that will be crucial to your success will depend on what your current goal is, but the 3 Ps, along with people and time, will always play a starring role. Luckily, Cathy had learned something from her time on the left—both as a slender person and as an overweight person. She realized why she was failing to maintain the weight loss she had worked so hard to achieve and knew was healthy and right for her—she hadn't been ready to be that slender person. Only after she spent time visualizing what her new life would be and would entail did she finally learn to enjoy every minute of it. "If only I'd thought it through," Cathy said to me, "I'd have realized I needed to prepare for the consequences of success."

Success is the quality of every moment of your life, your being. Success is not a definition, a place you can ever get to; it is the quality of the journey.

—Jennifer James

In the course of transforming your life into an utmost life, you will always be checking and correcting your vision of success so that you're ready to move on with boldness. If you don't, you'll be like Cathy, spending needless months redoing work that you've already completed.

Don't Let Success Get Old

Sometimes the achievement of a goal itself can be the change that you haven't foreseen. That is what happened to one of the greatest motivational thinkers of our time, Robert H. Schuller.

Robert Schuller says, "Set goals—and live. Avoid them—and the slow but certain seeds of dying will invade your life. Because I was goal-dominated, I was alive with enthusiasm when I turned thirty, then forty, and then fifty. When I hit sixty, I could see that before I hit seventy, I would have fulfilled my forty-year goal. I sensed a gradual drop in my level of enthusiasm for living. I felt the emergence of a foreign feeling that I could only define as 'growing old.' "

What did he do? He set himself new goals. It took a while, and it took the support of his family and his God, but when it was all over, he said, "I felt forty years old again." Even someone as purposeful, experienced, and directed as Robert Schuller needed to go back to the basics.

Making Success a Habit

Setting new goals is one of the best ways to plan for the unexpected pitfalls of success, but there are others that are a part of both planning for success and making success a habit in your life rather than an end point. These general principles help you to continue growing, continue expanding, continue giving and gaining. These are the things that will turn your life from a good meal into a glorious cuisine.

Beware of New Comfort Zones

I hope that your life is satisfying and rewarding, that you are content with yourself and what you are doing. But beware of mistaking contentment for acceptance. A passive acceptance of what you have is sometimes harder to spot when things are going well than when times are tough. It can sneak up on you when you're not on guard, and ultimately it can be more harmful than an obvious obstacle. It's what I call the boiled frog dinner. You know that old joke: how do you boil a live frog? If you fill a pot with water, bring it to a boil, and throw a frog in it, the frog will jump out, right? But if you fill the pot with water, put it on the stove, and put the frog in it, he'll just swim around and be happy.

Then you turn on the heat, but very low, so that the water gets hotter, but very, very slowly. If you do this carefully enough, the frog gets accustomed to the heat by degrees, and before you know it you have boiled frog for dinner.

That pot is a comfort zone that many of us find ourselves cooking in. That is, we get ourselves into a situation by degrees. You've found yourself a better job than you had before and you are appreciated at work. Or your old friends get jobs and get busy, and some of them move away, so you talk to them less and less because, well, your life has changed and their lives have changed.

Or you get into a relationship with someone who's not so bad, and you see your friends less and less, and you stop going to the gym so often, and you stop taking that class that you were taking. Then the relationship goes down the tubes and you're depressed, so you still don't go to the gym, or take the class, or see your old friends. You just sit simmering in your pot until one day you wake up and realize you're totally cooked. Your life isn't what you want it to be, and you don't see any way to get out of it or change it.

> *You will become as small as your controlling desire, as great as your dominant aspiration.*
>
> —James Allen

So even if you're not feeling that divine dissatisfaction, keep looking for new things to do, new ways to do them, and new people to enjoy them with. Change is constant, and the only thing you can do about it is to make sure that it is constantly in the direction that you want it to go.

One thing to remember is that you're not going to stop growing just because you've grown. Every goal that you reach provides the talent, the experience, and the excitement that makes you want to reach for the next one. Now that you're not bouncing up and down every time something good or bad happens, you'll be able to enjoy every meal for what it is, and also to envision a better one. Their variety and rewards are infinitely varied and unique. Enjoy where you are but keep on the way to where you're going.

Similarly, even though you're clear about your goals and how you plan to reach them, that doesn't mean you should stop thinking about them. As you gain knowledge, gain skills, gain confidence, you may realize that there are better or more rewarding ways to reach them. As you observe, research and study, investigate and navigate, you will learn more both about your goals and about yourself. A skill you have learned in one aspect of your life may be perfect somewhere else. You'll meet new people. They all have something to give you. Don't simply swallow new things that come your way. Chew them over, taste all the flavors that this new delicacy contains, and you may find that there are many ways to enjoy it.

I believe that the more you are able to change yourself, the more you will want to make your life a better place, but given the difficulties and challenges of life, the times on the left that will inevitably come, it's easy to say to yourself, *It's OK, I'll just hold here for a while.* Holding may be OK for a while, it may be necessary for a while, but make sure that it doesn't become a holding pattern. While a season on the left can make you stronger, time in a holding pattern will make you weaker.

Scientists say that the important difference between people who become champions and the people who study all their lives and remain amateurs is that the champions never stop learning from their mistakes and never stop challenging themselves to do something more difficult.

They may even spend a long time learning. Sometimes they will try things that are too hard and they will fail, but they will find a way to use that failure to succeed.

As long as you're green, you're growing; as soon as you're ripe, you start to rot.

—Ray Kroc

Even when you're creating the life you want, there will be times when you make choices whose consequences turn out to be different from what you expected. If they are wrong ones, move on—that is, go back and start over. But if it's not quite what you wanted, see if you can't make it so. Try adding a little salt or pepper or sugar or good olive oil or a sprinkling of cheese or pickled jalapeño peppers. You may find that the meal is a whole lot tastier than you expected.

Change your attitude

Maybe you have to have dinner with your relatives. You've begged and pleaded with your wife, but she's not letting you get out of it. You just can't stop thinking, *This is not going to be fun.* What if you said to yourself, *I have the power to make this fun. How can I do that?* If your wife's father thinks you're a lazy good-for-nothing, now you can let him know what you've been doing with your life. Even if you're in the same company or the same job, now you have a plan and a promise and a program. Maybe you can bring something special to the table that will change the whole atmosphere. You'll be amazed at how differently people will react to you when you are content with your life and eager to make it better, when you have confidence and a vision. It's a known fact that when people associate you with good times, they will like you better—and you'll like them better.

Take a break

If you're working hard on a difficult project and come to a point where you can't figure out what to do next, take a break. Try writing down the problem as clearly and concisely as you can—then go do something else. There are times when your subconscious will continue working on the problem. The next time you go back to it, a solution may appear. Of course, there will be times when just writing down the problem provides the solution.

Ask the experts

If you need to learn how to do something, find someone who has already done it, or something like it. Especially in these days of easy Internet access at libraries across the country, you can read and learn from experienced professionals, committed amateurs, and even other people who are trying to find out the same thing.

Get Outside the Box

This is another way to lift your life to a new level. You remember those activity books that you had when you were a kid? Well, the one I remember best had a puzzle that was a grid of dots, five rows of five dots. Inside it, some of the dots had been connected with short lines, but they were all going in different directions. The game was to connect three of the lines to make a triangle without lifting your pencil from the paper. Well, I puzzled over that one a long time. I really tried, but I just couldn't see any way of making a triangle out of these lines that were going such different ways. Finally, I looked at the answer—you may know what I found. In order to make the triangle, you had to draw the lines outside the square and then go back to it to form the triangle. You never lifted your pencil, but you didn't just stay inside the box either. I suspect that's where the phrase "Think outside the box" originally came from.

There's a wonderful book by Michael McMillan titled *Paper Airplane*. It's about an elementary school class that was studying the Wright brothers and the beginning of flight. They studied wings and streamlining and how airplanes are made. Then the teacher said they were going to make paper airplanes and see whose design would fly the farthest. Each child got a piece of construction paper and started folding the paper. Except for one kid named Jeff. Jeff just sat there thinking.

Finally everybody but Jeff had made an airplane and they all went outside to the playground to test out their airplanes. They flew them and they measured how far each one went. Except for Jeff. Jeff was still holding his piece of construction paper, which he still hadn't folded. He asked to go last, and the teacher said OK.

So when everybody else had flown their airplane, Jeff stepped up to the starting line. He held his piece of paper and looked at it. Then he wadded it up into a ball and threw it as far as he could, which was twice as far as any of the paper airplanes flew. The class went wild.

You can see why. Jeff had the ability to think outside the box (and also a flair for the dramatic). He was able to put aside the situation as it was set up and simply look at the goal and figure out the best way to reach it. Maybe he didn't make a paper airplane, but he did make a paper satellite.

All of us live in a variety of boxes, some of them large, some of them small. Money can be a box, for instance. You can become so concerned about money that you shortchange your own dreams. Your job can be a box, your family can be a box, your education can be a box, your past can be a box. Remember Carlos, who had never even asked his wife whether he should change careers? He was trapped in a box of his own making—and it may not have existed outside his own mind. When you are looking at your goal, try to break free of those boxes with a what-if. What if you had all the money in the world? What if you didn't have to support your family? What if you had an hour of free time in the middle of the day? When it comes to thinking, don't live within your means. No matter what the level of your ability, God has equipped you with more potential than you can use in a lifetime.

I'm not saying that you should run away and leave your family in the lurch, or that someone is going to knock on your door and hand you a check for a million dollars. But once you've played the what-if game and answered the question honestly to determine what you would do, then you keep on playing it to discover how you might get to that goal. You will probably want to get back into some of your boxes—the ones that are there because they fit you instead of restricting you. However, you may discover a way to open up your family box to accommodate your dreams.

Be Flexible

When we say something is flexible, we mean that it can be bent without breaking. Somebody once joked, "Blessed are the flexible, for they shall not get bent out of shape." Being flexible means being able to adapt to life's constant changes, to adjust yourself to fit a changing situation. Since we can't really predict how we will feel next month or even tomorrow, since we don't know what will happen in our job or with our friends or family from week to week, there will always be times when you have to readjust your plans and your priorities. That doesn't mean you've failed or faltered. Psalms 92:12 puts it like this: "The righteous will flourish like a palm tree." A palm tree is flexible. It will not break in winds of 160 miles per hour—that palm tree will bend and come back for more.

We love to fix the blame rather than fix the problem, but we can avoid a lot of trouble and disappointment if we look for new approaches when things don't go our way. Don't keep banging your head against the wall—go get a sledgehammer. If you rely on your abilities and your strengths, you can invest your energy in finding a new way to get over or around that wall rather than trying to get through it.

A wise man will make more opportunities than he finds.

—Francis Bacon

Being flexible applies as much to our own plans as to the walls that life throws into our paths. You should be setting goals and planning your future, but don't become so caught up in your plans that you can't take advantage of opportunities that come along. What's most important is that you are open to opportunities and ready to see the unexpected as an opportunity rather than an obstacle. Remember that God has a plan for you, and you never know when He's going to make it possible for you to act on it.

You may know the story of Gideon. He was the son of a farmer during a time when the land of Israel was under attack from the Midianites. One day he was supposed to be out in the field threshing wheat, but actually he was hiding in the wine press because he was afraid of the Midianites. The Lord came to him and told him to lead his people against their enemies, but Gideon wasn't so sure. "Wait a minute," he said. "How can I deliver Israel? My people are the weakest in the whole valley. Not only that, I am the least person in my family. I really think that you should look for somebody else."

God told Gideon that it was his time and it was His time, that Gideon had the strength and that He would give Gideon strength. And Gideon destroyed the Midianites. You never know what God has in store for you, so when something new comes along, don't jump into the wine press. Even if it seems as fearsome as a Midianite, it may be just the thing that will put you into the history books.

Opportunities are usually disguised as hard work, so most people don't recognize them.

—Ann Landers

Opportunities will present themselves, and you need to wear hope on your face when you're looking at them. Look for something to go right. Don't worry if you don't feel ready for it. You'll never be completely ready. If you wait until you think you're ready, it will be too late. So just be ready all the time. Opportunities won't always happen when you need them, so you need to prospect for them, as Robert Schuller says. You can do that by taking classes, perhaps, or by meeting with people who can help you. You can do it by keeping in touch with your friends who are thinking about the same things.

When an opportunity comes along, even if it's something you didn't foresee, inspect it. Take a good look at it; open your mind and your heart to it. Think about how much time and money it will take. But also think about how you may prosper from it. Respect that opportunity, and if it's the right one for you, select it. Keep looking for new challenges because they are the things that will make you stronger, healthier, happier. Once you start to settle into things, you get cemented. What you need to do is to break free from that cement and stay flexible.

Have Faith

Flexibility can go too far, of course, but as long as you trust in your God idea, you won't go too far wrong. That faith is your safety net. Although you may question what you've just done or what you did last week, faith in your God idea is your backbone, the steel rod that holds the building up.

We don't know everything, and sometimes we need the strength of a higher power. In the Old Testament, David said, "God is my refuge and my strength." There are infinite laws behind the universe, and no one is so strong that they don't need someone to take them by the hand from time to time. Have faith and enjoy the peace that comes from it. As Robert Schuller says, "Let go and let God."

God comes to you, picks you up, and takes you places that you never could have found for yourself. In high school, I never studied as much as I should, so I barely knew what Congress was. Then one day many years later I got a call from the U.S. Congress asking me to address Congress on "spiritual issues." By that time I was traveling and speaking quite a lot, and one of the people who heard me speak worked in the office of the Speaker of the House of Representatives, at the time Tom Foley.

I knew that she worked in government, but that was all; to me, she was just a good Christian who needed some help with a problem. I had no idea she would ever tell Speaker Foley about me. But she did tell him, and he did call me. For whatever reason, I was in the right place at the right time. And when the call came, I didn't jump into the wine press.

I was the youngest person to speak to Congress on spiritual issues since Billy Graham. Everything was formal. I stood in one corner while they introduced me. I couldn't believe I was there. I was quiet for a moment, thinking about my father and my sister dying, and my mother working double shifts in a donut shop. I felt that God was with me.

> *Not only are you responsible for your own life, but doing the best at this moment puts you in the best place for the next moment.*
>
> —Oprah Winfrey

Your destiny is all around you. Be observant and be creative. As you work with the tools and techniques we've discussed in this book, you will be better able to take advantage of opportunities. And as you develop your confidence, more opportunities will come, and you will be able to take full advantage of them.

- Plan for the consequences of success.
- Beware of new comfort zones.
- Keep readjusting your goals.
- If something goes wrong, don't just give up—see if you can adjust and refine.
- Get out of your boxes.
- Be flexible—inspect, respect, and select all the good opportunities that come your way, even when they're unexpected.

YOUR UTMOST LIVING JOURNAL

Make yourself a dream board or a success scrapbook: cut out pictures and stories about people who are living the life you want to live. Keep it where you can look at it or will pass by it many times a day. If you use a computer, make a screen saver of your dreams, in words or pictures that will remind you of the utmost life you will be living.

Start your personal record book. Every time you accomplish something—anything—that you haven't been able to do before, write it down.

Dream bigger. Look at the list of things that you never thought you would be able to accomplish. Imagine what you will need to make those dreams come true.

Pick a teacher for the day or the week. Think about someone who has a characteristic you admire—a friend, a relative, a colleague, or someone you've heard or read about. It could even be your pet or an object that you particularly cherish. Think about what you can learn from that person or thing.

Pick someone to appreciate once a week. Drop that person a note about how much you enjoy their company or admire their work. If it's someone you know, you'll be amazed at the warmth it will give to your life. If it's someone you don't know, you may be surprised at their gratitude.

11

. . .

From Most to Utmost

When we're building something, it's always helpful to have three things: a set of instructions about how to put it together, a picture of the final product, and a list of the things you can do with it. If you're building one of those radio-controlled model planes that the kids like so much these days, the first thing you need is the step-by-step instructions for assembling the pieces. At each step, you look at the picture of the final assembly and use that to help you understand the step you're on. Once you have it all together, you want to know how to start it, make it take off, maneuver, and land.

Since this book is about building an utmost life, it's only fair that I give you all three. Putting an utmost life together is the most complicated part of the process, and I've taken the largest part of this book to give you the tips, techniques, ideas, and guidelines that will help you attack any aspect of your life and begin to improve it. Your utmost life will be different from mine, but the steps are much the same for each of us. Now I'll try to give you a picture of the goal (that is, how it feels from the inside to be living an utmost life) and the rules for use (what aspects of life to focus on).

What does the final assembly look like, and how does it feel to be living an utmost life? Are people who are living an utmost life different from the rest of us? Do they jump into phone booths and rip off their clothes to reveal the Utmost costume underneath?

Contentment, Confidence, Commitment

You don't have to be a superwoman to live an utmost life. You won't start running a multinational corporation in your spare time. Anyone living an utmost life probably looks a lot like you and me—but it may feel a little different when you're actually around these people. What makes them different is their attitude, and it shows up in all kinds of ways. One of the things I see in people who are on the road to a better life is contentment. They can roll with the punches and they don't let the turkeys get them down. When something goes wrong, they don't panic or fall into a funk or get depressed. They are steady people to know; their moods don't swing wildly. That doesn't mean they can't be up, and in fact they usually are, because even if life isn't right most of the time, they accept it, use it how they can, and try to find the bright side.

They can be saddened by misfortune or illness, but when it happens to them, they deal with it as best they can. Frequently, the way they deal with the bad things involves the network of friends, family, and colleagues that they have nurtured around themselves. Just as often, they confide in God and ask for His help.

Another thing I see in successful people is confidence. They don't wonder if they are capable of achieving a goal; they know that they have or can acquire the personal tools or skill or knowledge that they need. That confidence is a great support for their contentment, and also for their persistence. When you have confidence, you are more likely to continue working at something past the point at which others quit. So instead of quitting just before they accomplish what they set out to do, these people will make that extra effort that puts them over the hurdle. They are confident because they have understood the promise that has been made to them and they want to see it fulfilled.

> *I'm a survivor. Being a survivor doesn't mean you have to be made out of steel, and it doesn't mean you have to be ruthless. It means you have to be basically on your own side and want to win.*
>
> —Linda Ronstadt

Of course they don't always succeed, but they learn from their failures. If they come in second, they study what the winner did. If they don't solve a problem, they ask someone else for help, or go back to do more research, or wait for the new idea that will inevitably come to them. When people criticize their work, they can see the help in the criticism and ignore anything that is useless to them—the kinds of comments that come from envy or jealousy. In some respects they can take the "me" out of the equation. They don't let their ego blind them to useful criticism or make them sensitive to useless criticism.

They have traded looking at the ground for looking at the sky.

Rather than expecting life to be the same day in and day out, they look for new opportunities and new ways to enjoy or exploit the old ones. As I say, they've raised the roof on their expectations and have a vision of life getting better and better rather than worse and worse. They know the wisdom of that old story—if there's a lot of horse manure around, there must be a pony nearby.

The only way to discover the limits of the possible is to go beyond them into the impossible.

—Arthur C. Clarke

At the same time, they've stopped chasing after butterflies and started digging for diamonds. Butterflies are beautiful but difficult to catch. Too often, talented, energetic, and enthusiastic people can get carried away with an idea that is simply impossible to accomplish no matter how much time, effort, knowledge, and inspiration they put into it. Those are people who are chasing butterflies. No matter what you do, a butterfly will get away from you, and it'll just distract you from your plan and your priority pathway. Instead, the people I know who are successful have switched to digging for diamonds. That is, you know where you can find diamonds—the characteristics of a diamond mine are generally well known. More important, you know that if you keep digging, you will eventually find what you want. Diamonds aren't going anywhere, so persistence will pay off in the end.

These are people who are fully engaged with the life around them. They have made a commitment to their life. Sometimes people say that they got into something too deep, but many people never get into life deeply enough. Those people are waiting for someone to tell them what to do, to tell them what's right, to tell them what to think. We usually think of "commitment" as meaning that you have pledged yourself to some effort, but there's another meaning, one that you hear in a sentence like "I commit my soul to God"—we mean we have entrusted ourselves to God, we trust that He will bring us to the proper, joyous end. These people are not waiting for the wind to blow so that they know which way to go.

> *You're not free until you've been*
> *made captive by supreme belief.*
>
> —Marianne Moore

They are people who don't trip over their own feet and who can stay out of their own way. When things are going well, they don't worry about an unexpected disappointment or a change in their life's weather. They have faced their fears and discovered the ways they can sweep them away. For instance, some people fear authority because their parents were demanding and withholding, but as they gain confidence and begin to succeed in their chosen vocation, they realize that their bosses want advice and help. And they have the confidence to know that losing a job doesn't mean the end of the world. They don't spend their time forcing themselves to do a task that they don't like. They may have accepted that their dislike of doing a particular kind of job comes from not being good at it. They may have found a partner who enjoys just what causes them anxiety or boredom.

They know where they're going on the inside. These are people who feel that they have a place in the world, and that they deserve that place. They've taken stock of who they are, given up the luxury of blaming others for their shortcomings, and acknowledged that other people have something to contribute to their lives. They know when to stop talking and start listening. They've also acknowledged that other people have faults and make mistakes, but they don't let other people's mistakes and faults preoccupy their mind and occupy their time. They understand that all people are imperfect. They can forgive and forget.

They are people who believe in themselves and their lives. Their success brings change and new challenges, but they know that is part of an utmost life. When you have that kind of faith in yourself, you'll want new challenges; you'll want to exercise your creativity and imagination again and again. You never arrive at the finish line in life; every finish line is the starting line for a new race, and when you're on your game, you're eager for that new race to start because you enjoy it so much.

> *Don't put off for tomorrow what you can do today, because if you enjoy it today you can do it again tomorrow.*
>
> —James Michener

Life isn't about satiating your hunger—hunger is about keeping you in pursuit of a good life. Remember that whatever it is you want to do, you have everything you need to do it. Your destiny is not a matter of chance, but a matter of choice. Success is a matter of a deliberate decision. Today's decisions are tomorrow's realities.

Utmost in Every Way

But what about those guides for use that I was talking about? If you want to make your life utmost through and through, where do you focus your attention?

First, people who are striving for an utmost life are looking beyond any single goal to a life that expresses their purposes in as many ways as possible. I hope the exercises and ideas in this book have shown you that there are always new levels of accomplishment and new worlds to conquer. As you become more confident in your ability to succeed, you will find that an idea that might have seemed a pipe dream only a few years ago can suddenly be something that is within your grasp. You are looking beyond today to tomorrow. You are looking beyond what you know now to what you hunger to know more about. You are raising the roof on your expectations and are happy to find new ways to fulfill them.

An appetite for change is the second characteristic of an utmost life, but it's not just change for the sake of change. You will be a different person when you accomplish your goals, but I mean that in a different way than we've discussed before. Yes, you will be a different person in that you've changed your habits, maybe changed the people you associate with, and probably changed your lifestyle in bigger or smaller ways. But you've also changed the limits of your potential—and that's the greatest change of all.

It's like you're climbing a ladder—with every step that you go up, you can see a little farther. At some point, you begin to be able to see things that you didn't even know were there. Not only will you be able to see them, you'll be able to touch them. In fact, you may be able to grasp a brass ring that you didn't even know was there. Achieving a goal, even a major goal, isn't the end of your story. As you banish negative thoughts, replace those bad habits with good ones, and envision the way you will be, you will begin to see that there is always another goal. In fact, having a new goal becomes part of the person you are.

I experienced that feeling not too long ago. In my work, even after I readjusted my priorities, I travel a great deal, mostly on airplanes. Anyone who spends a lot of time on airplanes inevitably spends at least some time reading the magazines on the airplanes. And not just sports magazines or newsmagazines, but everything—even the fashion magazines. I was admiring the clothes and some of the artistic jewelry for men and women, but for me there was something missing. The jewelry was often beautiful, but it didn't mean anything to me. For a deeply Christian person like myself, it didn't have any resonance. I know about all the traditional jewelry that people wear to proclaim their faith, but that wasn't the kind of thing I was looking for either. I thought that there might be other people like me who felt the same way.

We know what we are,
but not what we may be.

—Shakespeare

So I thought I'd take a shot at designing jewelry that would have meaning. I created a design that expressed the idea that good things are coming your way. I made some drawings and took them to a friend of mine who is a jeweler. Well, I have to say I was a little surprised, but not at all unhappy, when he said, "There's some real talent in these drawings. Let's try to manufacture a couple of these pieces."

There were more drawings, more meetings, and more talking with manufacturers. I started studying how silver and gold are crafted, which is something I'd never done before. I learned many new things—about the materials, about the business, and about myself. Through my persistence and my passion, I now have a jewelry collection, called Miracles for Me, that's going worldwide.

I was speaking at a motivational meeting in Los Angeles, and a lady came up and said, "Are you Tim Storey?" I said that I was, but she persisted: "Tim Storey, the jewelry designer?" I had to laugh. Here I'd spent years motivating people in one way or another and suddenly I was Tim Storey the jewelry designer, all because of my doodling on an airplane. You never know what you can become on the Anything Is Possible Network.

The third characteristic of an utmost life is that it is filled with love, beginning with yourself. Living an utmost life means seeing yourself with accuracy and appreciating what you see, as well as being excited by the prospect of what you can become. If you think you're ugly, if you're down on yourself, you can't love anyone else. Only when you have a basic self-regard can you connect with the people in your life.

Where there is love there is life.

—Gandhi

Fourth, an utmost life is a healthy life. You are physically fit. You don't feel tired when you wake up and you don't ache from sitting too much or from standing too much. I'm sure that when you were drawing up your list of goals, many of you had healthy goals near the top of your list—losing weight, exercising more often, cutting down on the foods and drinks that make you tired or weak. But if you didn't, there should come a time when you consider these as goals to be achieved. Many people don't like to see doctors, but a regular checkup is part of living a wise life.

Unhealthy living is not just bad for yourself, it's a burden to those who love you. They want you to live as long as possible, and they want you to live that life fully and with enjoyment. It's no fun to be bedridden, to have to walk with a walker, to have other people doing things for you, to be unable to do the physical things that you enjoy. This is a perfect example of how every dimension of our lives is connected to every other dimension. Our happiness is linked to the happiness of those we care for, and the times when we fall short always carom back to fall on them.

Fifth, you make leisure time for yourself and you enjoy it. This too is a fundamental part of so many other aspects of the utmost life, but few of us really take advantage of it. I have a friend—we'll call him Andrew—who has two grown sons. The boys are a mess, always getting into trouble, never at home, disrespectful, and without goals or hopes. Andrew is at a loss to explain it. He feels that he gave them the best life he could. In the beginning, money was tight and he felt his duty was to keep a roof over their heads. Now he's a terrific success in his business, but he's had to work at it seven days a week. He will admit that he's only been to the zoo once with his kids. He never played catch with them. He wasn't there for his kids. And now they aren't there for him.

> *My father gave me the best advice of my life. He said, "Whatever you do, don't wake up at sixty-five years old and think about what you should have done with your life."*
>
> —George Clooney

You can't relive the days you've lost, so treasure them every day you wake up. As in all things, there must be a balance in life. Enjoy your work, but enjoy your time with your family and enjoy time alone when you need to. God will not frown on it. As it says in Matthew 6:26–29, "Consider the fowls of the air: for they sow not, neither do they reap, nor gather into barns; yet your heavenly Father feedeth them. Are ye not much better than they? . . . Consider the lilies of the field, how they grow; they toil not, neither do they spin: and yet I say unto you that even Solomon in all his glory was not arrayed like one of these." It's such a beautiful verse, it's hard not to quote all of it.

Leisure is not, on the other hand, another kind of work. The dictionary says it plainly: leisure is "freedom from the demands of work *or duty*," and our word comes from an older one that means "to be permitted." Some people seem to think that they have to work as hard at having fun as they do at a job. They have to play in a softball league and win every game. Of course, it's just the opposite. Leisure is the time when you cannot lose. Just the doing of it is enough of a reward, and the relaxation it provides is like money in the bank. You will return to work and duty refreshed and reenergized.

> *There are two things to aim at in life: first, to get what you want; and, after that, to enjoy it. Only the wisest of mankind achieve the second.*
>
> —Logan Pearsall Smith

Sixth, your budget doesn't control your life. This is another way in which contentment is a fundamental part of the utmost life. I'm sure that many of you know how money can steal the soul out of your life. Money is the root of all evil, the Bible says, and we sometimes take that to mean only that people commit crimes or neglect their family and friends in order to get money. But there's another meaning to that phrase that we sometimes don't appreciate.

> *Life is not merely being alive,*
> *but being well.*
>
> —Martial

Working just to make money is an unfulfilling goal that can suck the joy out of your life. You may have seen the bumper sticker that says, "I owe, I owe, it's off to work I go," meant to be sung to the tune of "Heigh-ho" from *Snow White*. As much as I love Walt Disney, that bumper sticker always makes me mad, because if you are working just to pay off your debts, then you're working for the wrong reason. Of course you need to pay off debts, but you can do that in a job that you find rewarding and enjoyable.

Adjust your budget to fit your needs, or adjust your needs to fit your budget. Adjust your life to fit your paycheck. Set a limit for yourself that's realistic. You'll find that in the time you might have spent shopping and browsing, buying and trying and returning, you could have been earning the money so you could be burning those bills. You will live more—really live—with less. The most destructive aspect of our obsession about money is that it takes our focus away from the real objective. It can limit how far your imagination can stretch, and make you unconsciously lower your vision.

The seventh aspect is to have faith in yourself and in your potential. Recognize the wonder of the person you are. You—your mind, your body—are as miraculous as the most highly sophisticated piece of equipment. But you have to remember to turn it on. Sometimes I think we're like a nation of VCRs with our clocks blinking 12:00 because we can't figure out how to set them. Have faith in yourself, and have faith in the world of which you are a part.

> *Vision is the art of seeing things invisible.*
>
> —Jonathan Swift

So don't restrict your vision of life to the goals that you set when you started to reinvigorate your life. Once you've acquired new, positive visions to replace the old negatives, it will be like taking off blinders. You'll be able to look around, look up, and look onward. Do something different, go to different places. Don't sit in your favorite television-watching chair. If you spend one hour a day learning about a subject, in five years you'll be an expert. Make a five-year plan.

How do you do all this? Take your time. There is no timetable except the one you set for yourself. I want to see life coming out of your eyes. The most important step you need to take right now is to change your mind-set. Make a personal commitment to live life to the fullest.

- Utmost living touches every aspect of your life.
- Utmost living is a continuous pattern of challenge, growth, and accomplishment.
- Life is a marathon, not a sprint—you have time to accomplish what you need to do.

YOUR UTMOST LIVING JOURNAL

Dr. Edward Hallowell, an expert on anxiety and stress, has compiled a list of the twelve dimensions that make our lives full, rich, healthy, and long in a book entitled *Connect: 12 Vital Ties That Open Your Heart, Lengthen Your Life, and Deepen Your Soul.* While no one can tackle all of its points at once, it provides a fantastic checklist that you will want to look over from time to time to make sure that you are not neglecting a crucial aspect of your life. I have summarized the list and condensed it to ten points, but I am grateful to Dr. Hallowell for providing the blueprint.

1. *Family.* Talk to your parents, siblings, and relatives on a regular basis. Treat your immediate family with love and respect. Are you emotionally close?

2. *Friends and community.* Find time to enjoy with your friends and share your life with them. Find ways to support the community you live in.

3. *Work.* Do you feel a sense of worth from your work? Are you appreciated there? Do you feel a connection with your co-workers and company?

4. *Beauty.* Do you make room for beauty in your life? Take time to enjoy a favorite art form.

5. *History.* Try to see your part of the history of humankind, because we all have a part. Learn about the history of your country, town, and culture.

6. *Nature.* Spend time outdoors or indoors caring for plants or appreciating nature. Find a special place in nature that is healing to you.

7. *Ideas and information.* Try to learn new things often and be interested in new ideas and perspectives. Make the most out of your brainpower.

8. *Organizations and institutions.* Being a member of an organization or group provides a special kind of connection to the life around you.

9. *A higher truth.* Make time for spirituality in your life, either by reading or listening to CDs or broadcasts. Seek meaning and truth in your life in whatever way resonates with you.

10. *Yourself.* Meditate, have quiet time alone to think about what matters most to you. Are you comfortable with who you are?

1 2

. . .

Belief in an Utmost Life

There is one more aspect of an utmost life, and it is the one that is greater than all the others. Your spiritual life must enfold and encompass everything else. There is a dimension to your life that is fundamental to your daily needs, fundamental to your sense of contentment, and fundamental to your utmost life. That dimension is what connects you to the world you see and the world you cannot see. It allows you to accept the promise you have been given and to give back from the rewards you've achieved.

Getting Beyond Ourselves

As we reach higher levels of accomplishment, we realize that there are even higher levels, and that those are the ones that take us out of ourselves. The experts tell us that we can't really become fully human—

appreciate beauty, create art, feel compassion and love for others—if we are starving, sick, or without shelter. Our basic needs must be fulfilled, but once those basic needs are met, we are almost compelled to try to make ourselves better.

I believe that a similar thing happens when our basic needs for success, self-acceptance, contentment, and faith in the future are also met. For those who have really savored their life, that's when the impulse is born to reach out to the world and return what we have been given. We can't focus on the rest of the world until we've fulfilled at least some of our basic personal needs. At the same time, unless we turn our attention to the life beyond ourselves, we will never be fully human and fully alive.

About twenty years ago I used to go jogging in a park near my mother's house. I often saw a woman walking slowly and with difficulty, usually in old clothes. Some of the neighborhood kids made fun of her, which made me want to make her feel better. So I would say hi as I jogged by, and she would sheepishly say hi back. One day I took it upon myself to ask her how she was doing, and her face lit up because someone was talking to her. I found out her name was Diane, and I asked her where she worked. She told me she had a job in a factory bagging plastic forks, knives, and spoons. When I asked her how much she made, she responded, "Twenty-nine dollars and fifty-eight cents." I said, "Oh my, that's a lot! Can you imagine all the things you could do with twenty-nine dollars and fifty-eight cents?"

Two weeks later, I was jogging again and saw Diane. She ran up to me saying, "Guess what?" and pulled out her paycheck. It was a little higher than the last one. She was beaming, and I beamed right back at her. Then every time she'd see me in the park, she would have her paycheck with her, and every time it was a little higher. And she would say, "Can you imagine what I can do with this?"

As the years went on, Diane would begin to look for my children in the park. "Tell your dad how much money I made!" she'd say to them. Her clothes began to look better, and I even saw an improvement in the way she walked. While Diane didn't receive the greatest gifts in her life, she did the best with what she had. And she has given me a great gift.

The acquisition of things is never satisfying in itself. Many people try to prove otherwise, but you can see in the lives of famous people again and again that unless they are happy with themselves, they will not be happy with what they own or control. Money, fame, and power are never enough on their own. Bill Gates and Warren Buffett, two men whose combined fortune is probably the largest the world has ever known, have agreed to give away much of their wealth—probably the largest donation the world has known from individuals. Everyone feels the need to find something more.

> *The trouble with the rat race is that*
> *even if you win, you're still a rat.*
>
> —Lily Tomlin

I had never met Lee Iacocca, the man who turned around Chrysler and had written several best-selling books, but one day he invited me to his home for dinner. You can imagine what I felt. I was in awe of Lee Iacocca, and I couldn't figure out why he wanted to have dinner with me. Going to his mansion was like walking into a fairy tale. It was like a castle, grand in scale and grand in hospitality.

We had a wonderful dinner, and afterward he sat me down in the living room. Then he said something that astonished me: "Mr. Storey, tell me the secret of your success." Imagine Lee Iacocca asking for the secret of *my* success. He'd written books about being a success. But it turned out that was a question he always asked people; it was one of the subjects that most interested him. "I've watched your videos," he said. "It's amazing what has taken place." We had a wonderful discussion about success.

I learned many things, one of them being that you can get to the top of the mountain and still be looking for other mountains to climb. It reminded me of chapter 2 of Ecclesiastes, which says that you can acquire material things, but you'll still be looking for serenity or even just a rhythm to life. That was one of the things Mr. Iacocca was enjoying at that point in his life, not just conquering or being in charge of something, but having rhythm in his life. The evening was a great privilege for me.

What did I tell Lee Iacocca? I told him that I was a God-made man, and he smiled at that—he knows something about assembling things. That dinner conversation was a God idea that opened the door for me to spend numerous one-on-one sessions with Mr. Iacocca, talking with him about the principles of God's kingdom. It had to be God.

Acquiring money, fame, and power may be thrilling. They may seem like ends in themselves, but take a moment to think about what happens after we die. You can't take it with you, but what will you leave behind? Fame will fade, power will flow elsewhere, money will be spent. But the example that you leave will linger in everyone whose life you have touched.

Your parents may have passed on, but wouldn't you say they live on in you? I don't mean that you are like them or do what they do, but whatever they did, you are the reflection of them. They may have given you only negative examples, ways to avoid being, but they are still there. More likely they are there in subtle ways that you do not fully understand. But whatever happened between you, their legacy is what they've given you.

One of my friends, who plays football for the San Francisco 49ers, is also a longtime friend of Bill McCartney, the man who created the idea of the Promise Keepers. They would go out walking and McCartney would say, "I may be crazy, but I see stadiums filled with men." He wasn't crazy.

> *I'll tell you a great secret, my friend.*
> *Do not wait for the Last Judgment.*
> *It happens every day.*
>
> —Albert Camus

A few years later, stadiums all over America were filled with men, fifty thousand of them and more, holding hands, crying, hugging, and sharing their feelings. Men who had been wandering in darkness were stepping into their rightful place as leaders in their homes and communities. I've been in Sweden, Norway, and England and heard men talking about Promise Keepers.

Bill McCartney had a God idea, and now it belongs to the world. People with a God idea create ripples throughout the world. They are a stone thrown into the world's pond, and the ripples they generate will touch every shore. Rosa Parks had a God idea, but it was a simple one. She didn't want to sit in the back of the bus. Of course, this was in Alabama when segregation was the law of the land and blacks were expected to do what white people told them to do.

But it had been a long day, and Rosa Parks didn't want to have to sit in the bumpy, noisy, smelly, uncomfortable back of the bus. So she sat down in the front. Then a white man got on the bus, looked at this black woman sitting right up there in the front of the bus, and demanded that she move back. There was even room for him to sit anywhere he wanted, but what he wanted was for her to move. The bus driver stopped the bus and asked Rosa Parks to move, and she still wouldn't move. They called the police, and she still wouldn't move. So they put her in jail.

That was exactly what God wanted. Rosa Parks's unwillingness to move became a national issue and a national symbol. It helped to ignite the civil rights movement and change America forever. Secretary of State Condoleezza Rice has said, "If it weren't for Rosa Parks, I wouldn't be here."

Everything that happens in this world touches everything else. Those people who keep on growing further and further into their utmost life begin to see the interconnectedness of things, and realize that they are a grand and glorious part of a miraculous whole. They want to share what they have with others, to pass on knowledge, to help other people evolve from an almost life to an utmost life. They have realized that the more you give to others, the more you have of yourself. The more they give to others, the more their lives are enriched and enlarged. The more links they have forged with other people, the stronger are the supports that hold them up.

One of the ways in which they are most connected to the world is in acknowledging that there is a Higher Power that holds everything together and makes everything possible. And they have made that viewpoint the standard for their lives. They have let God's opinion of them take the place of man's opinion. This knowledge, this acknowledgment, is something that we usually call faith, but once you've understood it, it's not at all an uncritical acceptance of some story without proof. Thomas Edison said, "I know this world is ruled by infinite intelligence." Everything that surrounds us proves that there are infinite laws behind it. Everybody needs someone to take them by the hand from time to time. Enjoy the peace that comes from having faith.

Now is the time for you to think of how you can prosper in the greatest sense, in the widest field. What does it mean to really prosper? It means to grow stronger, to thrive, to gain—in wealth, in knowledge, in energy, in love—to the point that you can share with others. Ask yourself what you are gaining from your life—education, career, business, profession, marriage, family, organization, structure, art, relationship, reputation. Are you driven by a compulsion to excel, to improve, to create, to contribute? Or is this just because you don't have anything else to do? Of course it's fine that you are healthier, more prosperous, less tense, but once you've achieved that level of accomplishment, you will have unleashed an enormous amount of energy that you will want to use. Energy doesn't want to rest, to lie idle. It wants to be used. You can fritter it away, but only at a cost to yourself.

> *You will find as you look back upon your life that the moments that stand out, the moments when you have really lived, are the moments when you have done things in a spirit of love.*
>
> —Henry Drummond

Many people believe that the solutions to all your problems are on the inside, and I would agree that we can make changes in ourselves so that our thoughts become our words, our words become our actions, our actions become our habits, our habits become our character, and our character produces our destiny.

However, I also think that at the beginning of that process, there is something outside us, God, who gives us the promise and the power to make those changes, one by one and step by step. He is always there with us, if we will only open ourselves to Him. I hope that as you become more content, more in control, and more successful in your life, you will realize that you are only feeding from the wealth of a Higher Power. Why? Because you will be so amazed at what you can accomplish that you will understand that you had to have had that help. It's quite literally miraculous. We are all God's miracle waiting to happen.

The Utmost Source

Faith is the bedrock that makes all the other things not just possible but inevitable. Acknowledging that God has created you in order for you to succeed brings contentment. Accepting that he has made you a promise, given you promise, allows you to trust that even the time of your life that you spend on the left has a purpose and a meaning. You may bend, but you will not break. It is easier to have confidence in ourselves when we have confidence in God's power and love for us.

The story of Noah tells us how faith can take us beyond our five senses. Noah was nearing the end of his life when the Lord called him. He didn't want to start an immense new project; he wanted to collect himself and tie things up for the next life. He couldn't imagine that it would rain so much that the earth would be drowned. He didn't know how to build an ark. But by committing himself, by entrusting himself to God, he saved himself, his family, and all the creatures of the earth.

This story is telling us a couple of things. One is that if you commit to your God idea, things will happen to you that will astonish you. No matter what you can imagine, God will put you in charge of a project that you couldn't have ever imagined before. It will be so big that it seems ridiculous. Can you imagine Noah going into the Home Depot of his day and asking for thousands of board feet of lumber? And he was building this boat in the middle of dry land. Not only that, he didn't really feel like doing it, and nobody was there to help him. But despite all the evidence of his eyes and ears, he trusted in the Lord and committed himself to the project. He worked at it every day, and he kept working because he had a cause that was bigger than himself, even bigger than his family. There must be success beyond ourselves or we will be no more than ourselves. I've said that if you don't change, you'll never be more than you are now. It's also true that if you don't get beyond yourself, you'll never be more than who you are.

Noah didn't stop and worry about whether he was doing the right thing, he didn't doubt that his project was a worthy one, he didn't wonder if he was just wasting his time. Understanding that God has made a plan for you—for your own good—makes it easier to get off your own back. What you think of as a weakness may be a special kind of strength that He has given you. Your job is to find a use for it. You may disappoint yourself, but if you accept that even the disappointment is part of God's purpose, you see that it is a challenge that he has given you to overcome.

> *Walking, and leaping, and*
> *praising God.*
>
> —Acts 3:8

These days, whenever someone has an injury or a disability, we call it being "challenged." We are physically challenged, or mentally challenged. When I was a kid I was book-report challenged. (I think we should all be like Michael Jordan, who was failure-challenged.) *Challenged* is the right word, but we should know that we are all challenged all the time. God challenges you to be greater, stronger, and more giving. And He is building you inclined ramps to get over the challenge at the same time.

Some people come to their faith early, and some come to it late, but most all thinking people ultimately begin to see the pattern in the design. God's plan for you is so big that it would be overwhelming without His help. It's not about your ability; it's about God's ability to flow through you. In the natural world, it would be impossible, so you have to tap in to the supernatural. Go through the invisible door into faith and everything is possible.

Once I was on a speaking tour in Sweden, giving it all I had. I was staying with an older couple who had invited me to their small village, which was about eight hours from Stockholm and home to about a thousand people. I had been preaching all over Sweden, and I was really tired. I decided to take a nap. But suddenly I felt that God was speaking to me, saying I should find a bicycle and ride on down the road. Well, it wasn't the thing I had been most looking forward to doing, but when the Lord calls, I know it's time to jump.

So I went to the people I was staying with and said that I had to have a bicycle. They said it was too cold to go out riding, and asked where I wanted to go. They would drive me, they said. But no, God had said a bicycle and I had to have a bicycle, so they gave me a bicycle and I set off, not really knowing where I was going. All I knew was that I had to go, so I trusted myself to the Lord. So there I was riding along, on a child's bicycle with my big Afro, and I'm pedaling and it's really cold.

Finally I pedaled up to a young man who was sitting by a lake. He was just sitting there, smoking a cigarette and having a beer. The first thing he said to me was, "Do you like rock and roll?" My first thought was how interesting it was that God would wake me up to ride my bicycle to a lake and have someone ask me if I liked rock and roll. Anyway, I said that I did, and he said that his favorite band was the Rolling Stones. Little did I know that this chat would change a life.

We talked for a while, and finally he asked me what I was doing in this little town. I said I was a minister and I was speaking in town. When he heard that he said, "Oh my goodness. I am a backslider." He went on to say that he had walked with God but he recently had walked away. He was at the lake actually praying, "God, if You're real, I would like You to show me something." After we prayed together, he said he felt the presence of God, and he wanted to take me back to his house to meet his wife and his mother-in-law. "They won't believe what happened to me."

As soon as I walked in, his mother started shouting, "Tim Storey! Tim Storey!" It turned out that she had heard me speak in Stockholm and had said to herself, "I wish my son-in-law could meet a person like Tim Storey."

The affirmation of God's power gives you those feelings of self-worth that are so necessary to enlarging your vision and your understanding. Sometimes we have visionary heavyweights and character bantamweights; people who dream great dreams but don't have the character to make them a reality. God has a call on your life, but it has to be undergirded by character. The man I met by the lake felt that he had devalued himself—he'd become a discount version of himself. The real him was making a demand on the person he'd become, and he was ready for his comeback to utmost living.

Once you realize that God has created you the way you are and wants you to make the most of it, it's easier to accept yourself and to respect yourself. And once you do that, it's easier to accept and respect other people, with all their foibles or foolishnesses. Because you have to agree that what you think of as a foible or a flaw is part of God's plan;

it's there for a reason—a reason you may never understand because it wasn't put there for you. Someone else will make use of the uniqueness, whether as a challenge, as a model, or as a trial. Don't ask why; just appreciate the intricacy.

As I say, people who have understood the nature of the universe and the Power that holds it together don't necessarily look any different from you or me. Appreciating the awe-inspiring intricacy of the world and its people and admiring the richness and variety is an easy matter when you think of things from a God's-eye point of view. What you might have called evil or misfortune takes its place in the larger design, becomes a thread in the carpet.

There's a passage in Ephesians that says we should walk worthy of the calling we've received. "Walk worthy" means to honor, to give the full value of the call on our lives. An utmost God desires utmost children. For me, revelation of how much God values us led to the conviction that I should make the most of it. God had called me to step up to a higher calling, to live an utmost life through God's principles. Whatever language you use to express it, I hope that you too will enjoy the blessings and the bounty that life has to offer as you honor your life and the life around you.

- An utmost life is never complete until it involves sharing its gifts.
- Accepting God's opinion of you will lift your burden and give you even greater strength.
- Faith in God and faith in yourself will bring you to new heights.

YOUR UTMOST LIVING JOURNAL

Ultimately, I believe, an utmost life will always lead you to appreciate the miracle of life and the world and to accept that there must be a Higher Power that has put it together. The variety and richness of the gifts we have been given and the intricate connections between all of us are too amazing for it to be an accident. Whatever you call that Higher

Power, you can have faith in it and call on it regularly. Take some time, preferably every day, to do three things:

1. Be grateful. Acknowledge the gifts you have been given in your life and celebrate them.
2. Ask your Higher Power for help, support, and wisdom to assist you in your path to the utmost life.
3. Stop your own thoughts and listen to what your Higher Power is telling you through the actions, events, and thoughts in your life.

Conclusion
The Beginning

I hope that by now you have begun your new life. If not, at least you have the menu. The most useful thing you have is the work you've done yourself (or will do, if you're the kind of person who likes to read the whole recipe before you start cooking). There is wisdom in what you have written as a result of your work—you may even surprise yourself with the insight you've had. Keep these lessons in front of you.

Looking back at your first notes about your purpose, your passions, and your priorities will always be useful. But probably even more useful will be your record of the difficulties, the setbacks, and the ways in which you overcame each one. Remember, it's how you get through the times on the left that makes you strong enough to get through the times on the right.

But those notes are merely the beginning of your autobiography of success. Don't let it stop just because you've come to the end of this book. Write the best of your thoughts into your daily planner, your calendar, whatever you refer to at the beginning and end of the day. If you don't have one, get one or make one. The one you make may be the best. You need to change—you know that. Start by keeping a daily diary. Keep a record of what you do, what you like, what makes you sick. Take a look at it every morning and every evening—make time for that. You will find a way, your way.

I also hope you've seen the value of imagination, focus, and courage. While we've gone on to other topics since those ingredients were introduced, I'm sure that you find yourself using them again and again: visualizing how you want your life to be, focusing on the tools you need and the steps to take in order to get there, then jumping into your project with both feet, not heeding those who would stop you, and sweeping out any negative feelings that would hinder you.

This book is not just for a single reading. I hope you'll turn to it whenever you're feeling that you need a second helping, a little energy snack. Life is a marathon, not a sprint. You will find that living an utmost life touches every moment of your day. Keeping your balance is a crucial part of that, as we've seen. You learn how to set your goals and your guides, to steer by your purpose, to accelerate on your passions, to use your priorities to plan the sequence of the route. But that route will change and grow, and you may find that touching on the ideas here again will have new value.

The goal of this whole book is really to make you turn those techniques into habits in your life. We've used dieting many times as an example, but it's almost always a good one. People lose weight on a diet plan, but before long—even if (or because) they've lost weight—they go back to their usual habits: a little extra here, a candy bar there. What you want to do is to develop habits. Habits of action are important, but even more important are habits of attitude. Ultimately, it's all in your attitude. If you believe in yourself and you believe in your purpose, you will make your goal a reality.

We've talked a lot about success and achievement and about setting goals and reaching them. But remember that not every goal is about acquiring things; not every success can be counted on your fingers. I believe that we often lose sight of what real success and real significance are.

You'll remember that saying: thoughts become words, words become actions, actions become habits, habits become character, character becomes destiny. I want your destiny to be one of success and of significance. I want those habits of vision, affirmation, and courage to become your hallmark, your trademark, so that everyone can see who you are and say, "This is a person who sees the truth and lives it. This is a person I want to be like."

That success and significance will be most glorious when they are as much about other people as they are about yourself. Television, movies, and advertising all surround us with pictures and tell us that we should own this thing or we should be like that person, that success can be measured in dollars and significance measured in sound bites. I've been behind those images, though, and the truth is often very different. The people who live for affirmation outside themselves never seem to have enough—enough fame, enough applause, enough love.

People who have seen that success comes from who they are don't need the admiration of multitudes. People who give to others know that they've accomplished something. People who have helped someone else's life know they have made their mark on the world. There are many ways to do that, large and small. Being a good father or mother or friend is one of them.

The way I think of it, your Father knows who you are and loves you. He loves you enough not to let you stay where you are, curled up in a little ball inside yourself. But it's up to you to take advantage of His love. It's not a wimpy kind of thing, you know. It's not like you sit around and say, "Now God, could you *please* get down here and help me out a little?" In fact, it's a power beyond our understanding that can make you feel like David with Goliath at his feet. But still, it's a power we can take advantage of.

On the next page, you will find a document that can mark the beginning of your utmost life: The Contract for Utmost Living. Look it over, and if you're ready to embark on this marvelous journey, ask a friend to be the witness to the launching of your new life. Making it public that way will jump-start the whole process. It's up to you. Your assignment is to become wonderful—to make the wonder that's in you come out. Let me know what happens. Let's celebrate together.

The Contract for Utmost Living

I, _____, hereby commit to live my life to the utmost.

- I will discover my purpose in life, unleash the power of my passions, and use my priorities to guide me.
- I will acknowledge that there is no limit to what I can achieve if I focus on my goal, use my imagination to plan how to reach it, and persist in my efforts until I achieve it.
- I will savor every moment of my life by thinking about, speaking of, and acting in the path of my utmost life.
- I will accept the setbacks life hands me and use them to raise myself to greater strength.
- I will affirm that whatsoever I receive in my utmost life, I will give in equal measure to others.
- I will believe in myself and in the higher power that will help me.

I make this contract binding with myself, knowing that its rewards or penalties will reflect only my own strength, vision, and character.

_____   _____

Signature   Date

I have witnessed this contract and support its fulfillment.

_____   _____

Witness signature   Date

Acknowledgments

To Nate and Al's in Beverly Hills—thank you for providing an atmosphere to help me observe and realize that life is like a diner.

To my manager and friend Suzanne de Passe, one of the smartest minds I know. Your leadership and skills are getting me heard and read.

To Alan Nevins of the Firm—you've believed in this project from the beginning. Your wisdom, strength, and humor have helped make this dream a reality.

To Lance Klein from Endeavor—you've been a great agent and friend, and you have always encouraged me to keep on keeping on.

To Quincy Jones, Lee Iacocca, and Bernie Brillstein—my mentors, who have stretched me through great conversation.

Thank you to my family, who have truly been a family to me. You've cared, loved, and believed at all times . . . especially you, Mom.

To my children, Isaiah and Chloe, who make me want to succeed so that they can have an easier path.

To Walt Bode, the best writing partner a person could have. Your love of life came through. You pushed me as a writer to my utmost level. You're a pro, Walt.

To my staff—thank you for your time, care, and belief in the power of making lives better.

To Julia Pastore—your dedication, hard work, and belief in this book will, in turn, change thousands of peoples' lives. Thank you for your constant care and consideration.

To the staff at Harmony Books—you've been a fantastic crew. I've enjoyed working with all of you.

Finally, to a most awesome God, who let me tell Bill Cosby jokes to Him while I rode my Schwinn bicycle when I was eight, and who has gifted me to see people through His eyes—wonderfully made and beautiful. You took a young boy with an almost life, and taught me it was possible to live at an utmost level.

About the Author

TIM STOREY is an acclaimed speaker, writer, and life coach. He has inspired and motivated people of all walks of life, from athletes, entertainment industry executives, and celebrities to adults and children in the most deprived neighborhoods in the country. Since receiving his doctorate of divinity from Bethany Theological Seminary, Tim Storey has visited fifty-five countries and spoken to millions of people. He is the author of several books, notably *It's Time for Your Comeback,* and has hosted a set of motivational audiotapes, *Personal Renovation.* He has also begun design and production of a jewelry collection with inspirational themes, called *Miracles 4 Me.*

Visit the author at www.TimStoreyOnline.com.